HANDS-ON HISTORY!
ANCIENT INDIA

DISCOVER THE RICH HERITAGE OF THE INDUS VALLEY AND THE MUGHAL EMPIRE, WITH 15 STEP-BY-STEP PROJECTS AND 340 PICTURES **DAUD ALI**
CONSULTANT: NICK ALLEN

ARMADILLO

This edition is published by Armadillo,
an imprint of Anness Publishing Ltd,
Blaby Road, Wigston, Leicestershire LE18 4SE;
info@anness.com; www.annesspublishing.com

If you like the images in this book and would like to
investigate using them for publishing, promotions or
advertising, please visit our website www.practicalpictures.com
for more information.

Publisher: Joanna Lorenz
Managing Editor, Children's Books: Gilly Cameron Cooper
Editors: Joanne Hanks, Louisa Somerville and Edel Brosnan
Copy Editors: Gill Harvey and Lucy Doncaster
Designer: Caroline Reeves
Illustrations: Stuart Carter, Chris Forsey, Rob Sheffield
  and Clive Spong
Special Photography: John Freeman

Anness Publishing would like to thank the following children
for appearing in this book: Emma Franklin, Samara Edwards-
Amos, Louis Jade, Adam Keevash, Christina Malcolm-Hansen,
Ivelin Nedkova, Thaddius Rivett, Luke Stanton

PICTURE CREDITS
b = bottom, t = top, c = centre, l = left, r = right
AKG: 9tr, 16tr, 16cl, 31tl, 33br, 34bl, 40tl, 46cr, 47cr, 47tr,
47cr, 51br, 54tl, 56c, 57tl, 51br, back cover, front cover; The
Ancient Art and Architechture Collection Ltd: 5ct, 14t, 14b
15tr, 20bl, 34br, 34tl, 44bl; 50br, front cover; The Bridgeman
Art Library : 4tr, 5tl, 11c, 11tl, 15bl, 17tl, 17tr, 17c, 18cl, 19c,
19tr, 19cl, 20tr, 21tl, 22tr, 27c, 29tr, 28cl, 31c, 32tl, 33tl,
33tr, 33bl, 35tl, 35cr, 36tl, 37tl, 40cr, 41tr, 43tl, 43tr, 43cl,
46tl, 46cl, 48tl, 49tl, 51tr, 51cl, 53c, 55tl, 54b, 58cr, 59tl,
59c, 60cr, 60cl, 61tr, title page; back cover; Corbis: 2t, 3bl, 4cl,
15br, 21br, 28tl, 38tr, 44br, 45b, 55tr, 56tl, 57cl, 58tl, 60tl; C
M Dixon: 3tr, 8tl, 10c, 44tl, back cover; E T Archive: 9c, 10tr,
26tl, 29tl, 43bl,45tl, 47cl, 52cr, 53tr, 52tl, 55cr; Mary Evans
Picture Library; 25bl, 26c; FLPA: 37c; Robert Harding: 24b,
25tr, 5br, 38b, 39bl, 42tl, 55b; The Hutchison library: 15tl,
23tr, 25tl, 42bl, 48cr, 59tr; Images of India: 20br, 22b, 21tr,
22b, 41tl, 41cl, 41c, 61cl; Philadelphia Museum of Art: 18tl;
Ann and Bury Peerless: 9tl, 45c; Link Picture Library: 5c, 23br;
V & A Picture Library:12t, 23bl, 24t, 29c, 30tl, 30cl, 37tr,
49cl; Oxford Scientific Films: 35bl; Royal Asiatic Society: 49c;
Tony Stone Images: 15c, 23 tl, 27t.

Manufacturer: Anness Publishing Ltd, Blaby Road,
Wigston, Leicestershire LE18 4SE, England
For Product Tracking go to:
www.annesspublishing.com/tracking
Batch: 1673-22514-1127

CONTENTS

The Glory of Ancient India

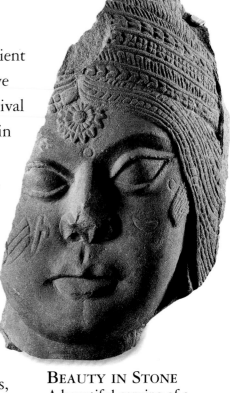

THE INDIAN SUBCONTINENT IS HOME to one of the world's most ancient and varied civilizations because many different groups of people have journeyed over the Himalayan mountains and settled there. From the arrival of Aryan tribes about 3,000 years ago until the invasion of the Mughals in the 1500s, each new wave of people brought fresh ideas and ways of life. As a result, India's religious and artistic life became very rich and mixed.

Two major world religions – Hinduism and Buddhism – developed in ancient India, and for hundreds of years, India was also at the heart of Muslim life in Asia. These three religions shaped the course of India's history, and led to the building of magnificent monuments, many of which still stand.

With its Hindu and Buddhist temples and sculptures, and the sumptuous palaces of the Muslim rulers, India is full of amazing treasures from the past.

DAWN OF INDIAN CIVILIZATION
Ancient stone buildings, such as the Great Bath at Mohenjo-Daro in the Indus Valley, tell archaeologists a great deal about the dawn of civilization in India. Fewer buildings of later times have been excavated, partly because later houses were made of mud, thatch and wood, none of which has survived.

BEAUTY IN STONE
A beautiful carving of a Yakshi (tree spirit) from Bharhut in central India. It is made of red sandstone and dates from 100BC. This Buddhist sculpture has a distinctive Indian style that you can see in sculptures from much later periods. Buddhism was the first religion in India to inspire people to build monuments and make sculptures.

TIMELINE 6000BC–AD400

From early times until the coming of the British in 1757, India was divided into many kingdoms. It was never a single state. The regions of Ancient India were linked by a common culture, rather than by politics, religion or language.

c. 6000BC Neolithic settlements in Baluchistan.

c. 2800–2600BC Beginnings of settlements in the Indus Valley region.

statue of priest king from Indus valley

rice cultivation

c. 2300–1700BC The great cities of the Indus Valley (Mohenjo-Daro and Harappa), the Punjab (Kalibangan) and Gujarat (Lothal) flourished.

c. 1700BC Sudden and mysterious decline of the Indus Valley civilization.

c. 1500–1200BC Immigration of Vedic Aryans into north-western India.

c. 1200–600BC The Vedic texts are composed.

c. 800BC Use of iron for weapons and the spread of Aryan culture into the Gangetic plains.

c. 500–300BC Rice cultivation and the introduction of iron for the use of agriculture in the eastern Gangetic plains lead to the formation of more complex societies, cities and states.

fragment of pot with brahmi inscription

6000BC   2500BC   1200BC   500BC

TEMPLE OF THE SUN
A huge carved stone wheel forms a panel on the wall of the Sun Temple at Konarak on India's east coast. This part of the temple is carved in the shape of a gigantic twelve-wheeled chariot, drawn by seven stone horses. It dates from the 1200s, when medieval Hindu kings built magnificent temples to their gods.

GRAND ENTRANCE
The Alamgiri Gate is one of three magnificent entrances built by the Mughal emperor Aurangzeb to the Shahadra fort at Lahore (in modern-day Pakistan). The fort doubled as a luxurious palace.

LIFE STORY
A limestone frieze dating from AD100 shows a good deed carried out by the spiritual leader, Buddha. The frieze comes from Amaravati, in south-eastern India, which was an important Buddhist site from 300BC. Stories of the Buddha's past lives, called *jatakas*, were popular in ancient India.

A COUNTRY OF MOUNTAINS AND PLAINS
India is bounded to the north by the Himalayan mountains. The central Deccan plateau is framed by mountain ranges known as the Eastern and Western Ghats. The first settlements grew up near rivers on the fertile plains in the north.

c. 500–400BC Inscribed fragments of pots from Sri Lanka discovered.

c. 478–400BC Life of the Buddha. He is born a prince but leaves his family to live in poverty.

327–325BC Alexander the Great arrives in north-western India.

coin of Alexander the Great

320BC The rise of the Magadhan empire under the Maurya family, founded by King Chandragupta I.

268–233BC King Ashoka, the grandson of Chandragupta I, issues the first royal edicts on pillars and rocks throughout the subcontinent.

c. 50BC–AD100 Intensive trade connections with Roman Empire.

AD50–AD200 Kushanas and Shakas (tribes from Central Asia) set up kingdoms and adopt Indian religions. Indian dynasty of Satavahanas arises in southern India.

Ashokan pillar

c. AD150 Kushana and Shaka kings in the north and west adopt Sanskrit as the courtly language.

c. AD200–400 *Ramayana*, *Mahabharata* and the *Bhagavad-Gita* Hindu epic poems are composed in their final form.

AD400 Nearly all courts are using Sanskrit.

gateway to Buddhist stupa

300BC AD100 AD400

The Land of Ancient India

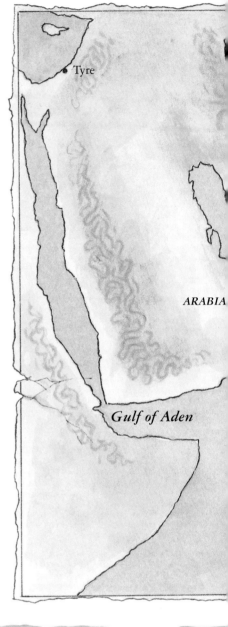

INDIA IS ISOLATED FROM THE main continent of Asia by the world's highest mountains, the Himalayas. The mountains made it difficult for people to invade. The easiest overland route, taken by the earliest settlers from Asia, is from the north-west (present-day Afghanistan) through the Karakoram mountains. However, it was still a difficult journey. Once people had arrived in India, they tended to stay.

The first people settled in the bare mountain foothills, and survived by keeping herds of animals such as sheep and goats. People gradually moved south of the Himalayas, to areas where mighty rivers run through huge, fertile plains. Here, the climate enabled them to grow various crops.

India's climate is dominated by the monsoon, a wind that brings alternating seasons of hot, dry weather and heavy rain and flooding. In the drier west and north, wheat was the main crop from very early times, while higher rainfall in the east and south was ideal for growing rice. Rice cultivation was so successful in the plains around the Ganges river that many people settled there. This led to the growth of cities from around 300BC. Later, cities developed along rivers farther south.

From the 1st century AD, people no longer needed to make the overland journey into India. They came by ship from as far away as the Mediterranean Sea to ports on the west coast, in search of trade.

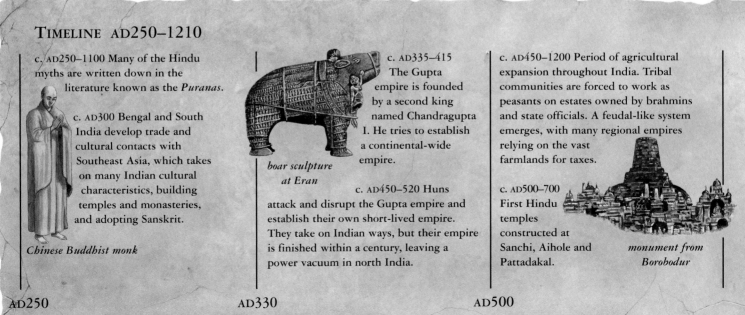

TIMELINE AD250–1210

c. AD250–1100 Many of the Hindu myths are written down in the literature known as the *Puranas*.

c. AD300 Bengal and South India develop trade and cultural contacts with Southeast Asia, which takes on many Indian cultural characteristics, building temples and monasteries, and adopting Sanskrit.

Chinese Buddhist monk

boar sculpture at Eran

c. AD335–415 The Gupta empire is founded by a second king named Chandragupta I. He tries to establish a continental-wide empire.

c. AD450–520 Huns attack and disrupt the Gupta empire and establish their own short-lived empire. They take on Indian ways, but their empire is finished within a century, leaving a power vacuum in north India.

c. AD450–1200 Period of agricultural expansion throughout India. Tribal communities are forced to work as peasants on estates owned by brahmins and state officials. A feudal-like system emerges, with many regional empires relying on the vast farmlands for taxes.

c. AD500–700 First Hindu temples constructed at Sanchi, Aihole and Pattadakal.

monument from Borobodur

AD250   AD330   AD500

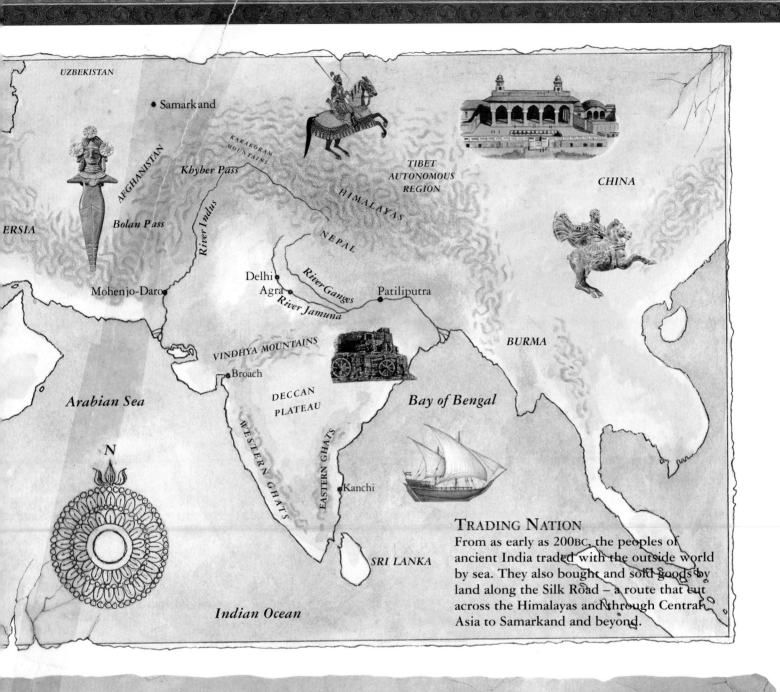

UZBEKISTAN

• Samarkand

AFGHANISTAN

KARAKORAM MOUNTAINS

Khyber Pass

TIBET AUTONOMOUS REGION

HIMALAYAS

CHINA

PERSIA

Bolan Pass

River Indus

NEPAL

Mohenjo-Daro•

Delhi•
Agra•
River Jamuna

River Ganges

Patiliputra•

BURMA

VINDHYA MOUNTAINS

•Broach

DECCAN PLATEAU

Bay of Bengal

Arabian Sea

N

WESTERN GHATS

EASTERN GHATS

•Kanchi

SRI LANKA

Indian Ocean

TRADING NATION

From as early as 200BC, the peoples of ancient India traded with the outside world by sea. They also bought and sold goods by land along the Silk Road – a route that cut across the Himalayas and through Central Asia to Samarkand and beyond.

AD606–647 Harshavardhana, king of Kanauj, visited by Hsiuen-tsang. Splendours of courtly life and medieval culture flourish.

c. AD630-643 Chinese monk Hsiuen-tsang visits India to find Buddhism in decline in some areas.

Krishna dancing on serpent

c. AD712 Arab conquest of Sind by Muhammad Ibn Qasim after the local king refused to punish pirates who had abducted a shipful of orphans sent by the king of Sri Lanka to Baghdad.

c. AD752 King Dantidurga establishes a powerful empire in the Deccan, which is recognized by Arab geographers and voyagers as one of the most powerful kingdoms in Asia.

Kailasanath temple at Ilora

AD997-1030 Sultan Mahmud of Ghazni makes 17 raids into northern India to loot temples of their wealth.

c. AD1077 Embassy of merchants from the Chola dynasty of South India arrive at the Sung court in China.

AD1206 Aibak establishes the Sultanate in Delhi, the first Muslim kingdom in India.

AD700   AD900   AD1210

History Makers

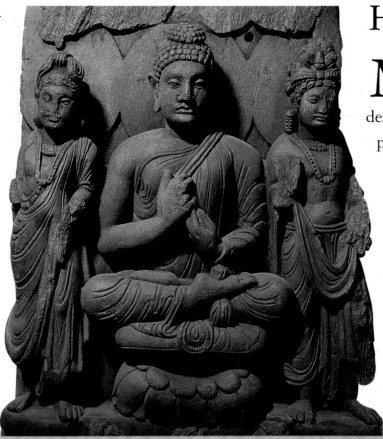

AN INFLUENTIAL LEADER
A statue of Gautama Buddha seated on a lotus flower. He founded Buddhism, which shaped life in India for thousands of years. Buddhism eventually died out in India, but it spread through many other parts of Asia. This created a link between India and many different eastern peoples and cultures.

MANY OF THE REMARKABLE FIGURES of Indian history who shaped the country's destiny were great leaders. Ashoka was a powerful ruler in the 3rd century BC, who encouraged the spread of Buddhism. Babur, a warlord from Samarkand in Central Asia, founded the Mughal Empire in India in the early 1500s. His grandson, Akbar, was a gifted politician and soldier who ruled for 49 years. The Mughal period was a time of huge development in the arts. Some Mughal rulers built magnificent cities, and many of their fine monuments and royal tombs can still be seen today.

From the time of the ancient civilization of the Aryans in the Indus Valley, religious teachers and scholars were respected. This may be because poverty and suffering have always been problems in India, which led people to think about why life was so difficult, and to seek ways of coping. Two of the most famous religious leaders are Gautama Buddha, who established the Buddhist way of life, and Guru Nanak, who founded the Sikh religion.

TIMELINE AD1290-1875

AD1293 Marco Polo visits South India. A flourishing trade is conducted throughout the Indian Ocean in silks, fabrics, spices and other luxuries.

AD1334-1370 The sultanate of Madurai, the southernmost Muslim kingdom, established briefly in south India before being defeated by southern kingdoms.

stone chariot from Vijayanagar

c. AD1346–1565 The last great Hindu empire of Vijayanagar founded in south India.

c. AD1360 Vedic and Hindu revival by the brothers Sayana and Madhava at the Vijayanagar court.

AD1398 The Mongol Timur devastates Delhi.

c. AD1440 Death of the Bhakti saint Kabir at Gorakhpur, where both Hindus and Muslims claim him as a great teacher.

tomb from the Sultanate period

AD1469-1539 Life of Guru Nanak, founder of Sikhism.

AD1498 Portuguese explorer Vasco da Gama visits Calicut.

AD1510 The Portuguese conquer Goa.

Qutb Minar marble fountain

AD1290   AD1340   AD1400   AD1520

ROYAL HANDWRITING

This signature of Emperor Harsha (AD606–647) is carved in copper. Harsha was a patron (supporter) of arts and literature, and during his reign, the richness and elegance of the court reached new heights.

A SAINTLY LIFE

A statuette of Karaikal Ammaiyar, a woman who lived in southern India around AD600. She was so devoted to the god Shiva that she left her home and family, and gave her life entirely to him. She fasted as a symbol of her faith and became incredibly thin. Karaikal Ammaiyar is revered as a saint even today in southern India.

ASHOKA'S PILLAR

An edict (order) of Ashoka, the ruler of India's first empire, is inscribed on this pillar. He published his edicts on pillars and rockfaces throughout the land. Ashoka was a Buddhist. He claimed to have improved the lives of humans and animals, and had helped to spread justice.

ART LOVER

Shah Jahan was one of the greatest statesmen of the Mughal Empire. He extended Mughal power south into the Deccan plateau and north into Afghanistan. However, he did not fulfil the Mughal dream of capturing the trading city of Samarkand, the 'blue pearl of the Orient', in Central Asia. Shah Jahan was a great patron of architecture.

AD1526 Babur, the Mongol, defeats the Sultan of Delhi and founds the Mughal empire.

AD1556-1605 Reign of Akbar, the most enlightened Mughal emperor.

Mongol horseman

AD1739 Nadir Shah sacks Delhi and carries off the Peacock Throne.

palace at Phata Pursi

AD1758 After defeating the Nawab of Bengal a year earlier at Plassey, the British East India Company for the first time receives from the Mughal rulers the right to collect land taxes in Bengal.

AD1857–8 British crown imposes direct rule and the East India Company is dissolved.

AD1870 Construction of Red Sea telegraph brings a direct link with Britain.

farman (order) of Mughal emperor to East India Company

AD1750

AD1850

AD1875

The First Indian Civilization

IN THE 1920s, archaeologists made an astonishing discovery. They found the remains of two great cities near the Indus River in north-western India. The cities were called Mohenjo-Daro and Harappa. Before this, no one had known very much at all about India's earliest history, but it was now clear that there had been a vast urban civilization in the area as far back as 2600BC, and that it had lasted for nearly a thousand years.

These ancient cities were very well organized. They had drainage systems, a network of roads, granaries, water tanks and canals, as well as raised citadels (fortresses) where the rulers lived. It is clear that the city dwellers traded with other civilizations, too, because Indus valley objects have been found as far away as Egypt and Mesopotamia. For some reason, this bustling culture declined after 1700BC. It is possible that the climate became drier, causing crops to fail, or that the people destroyed their own environment, perhaps by overgrazing. No one is sure.

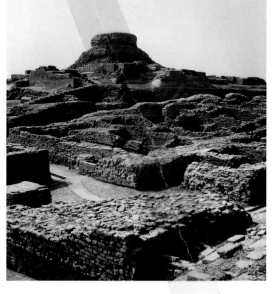

LOST CITY
Ruins of the citadel at Mohenjo-Daro. Like all the cities of the Indus Valley civilization, Mohenjo-Daro had a lower city and a high citadel. It was probably the largest of the Indus Valley cities. The raised stump at the back of the picture is the remains of a *stupa* – a monument containing relics of the Buddha. The *stupa* was erected long after the city declined.

TRADING TOKEN
Seals cast from soft soapstone may have been used as tokens for trading goods. This one shows a humped bull, or zebu. It comes from Mohenjo-Daro, and is over 4,000 years old. The symbols on the seal may have identified traders.

MAKE A CLAY SEAL

You will need: rolling pin, self-hardening clay, board, ruler or measuring tape, blunt knife, scrap paper, pencil, modelling tool, white glue, paintbrush, white paint, string, plastic oven-drying modelling material.

1 Use the rolling pin to roll out the self-hardening clay. When you have finished, you should have a rectangle-shaped slab of clay about 2cm/1in thick.

2 Carefully trim away the edges of the slab of clay so that they are neat and even. Your rectangle should now measure 10 x 7cm/4 x 3in.

3 Draw an animal shape on to the clay. (Practise drawing the shape on scrap paper first.) Carefully cut the pattern into the clay using a modelling tool.

CLAY WOMAN

A terracotta figurine from Mohenjo-Daro shows a woman in a headdress. The headdress looks as if it was made up of two baskets – a way of carrying heavy loads in India even today. The statue may have been a mother goddess or a doll or toy. Archaeologists have found groups of clay figurines such as this that show people doing things in and around the home.

DESERTED VALLEY

Today, the Indus Valley is no longer a fertile place in which people grow crops, but an arid (dry) landscape of bare soil. Around 1700BC, the cities of the Indus Valley were suddenly and rapidly depopulated. It is believed that a change in the course of the Indus River may have disturbed the primitive irrigation system, and led to a collapse in agriculture.

STORING FOOD

Large storage jars were used to keep and distribute food that was grown around Mohenjo-Daro. The fact that its people were able to store surplus food shows how settled and organized the society was.

INDUS VALLEY DANCER

This copper statuette shows a dancer from Mohenjo-Daro. It has an elaborate hairstyle, necklaces and lots of arm bangles. Thousands of years later, hairstyles and adornments such as this are still the ideal of what makes a woman look beautiful in India.

4 Roll out a 2cm/in sausage-shaped piece of self-hardening clay. Bend it into a curved handle shape. Glue this to the slab.

5 Paint the clay slab with a single coat of white paint. This will give your seal a clean surface that will not stain or leave any dirty marks.

6 Loop the string through the handle of your seal. Knot the string to secure. Form the plastic oven-drying modelling material into a slab shape.

7 Press the seal into the modelling material. Your pattern appears raised in reverse. Bake the material, following the instructions on the packet.

The Noble People

A KING AND HIS PRIESTS
A raja (king) consults his Brahmin priests near a sacrificial fire. The relationship of the Brahmin and the raja became very close in the time of the Vedic hymns. Brahmins performed the sacrifice for the raja in order to bring him wealth, prosperity and sons. When empires began to form after about 350BC, the Brahmins became the ministers of the king's government because of their important role.

ABOUT 400 YEARS after the decline of the Indus Valley civilization, a new wave of people arrived in India from the north-west, probably from central Asia. They were known as the Aryans, or 'noble people'. They lived in small groups or larger tribes. Gradually they moved farther into India and took over the part of the plains between the Indus and the Ganges rivers.

At first, the Aryans lived by herding animals, but as they settled, they started growing crops instead.

The Aryans divided society into three castes (classes). These were made up of priests (Brahmin), warriors (Kshatriya), and property holders (Vaishya). There was a also a fourth caste of servants and workers called Shudra, made up of the people that the Aryans had conquered. Each of the castes played a different role in an important Aryan custom – the offering of a burnt sacrifice of meat and grains to the gods in return for rains, wealth and sons. The hymns of praise to the gods during this sacrifice were called the Vedas. They were composed in a language that came to be known as Sanskrit, meaning refinement. These Aryan customs and writings formed the basis of the Hindu religion.

OFFERING CUP

You will need: Plastic drinking cup, scissors, piece of medium card, white glue or tape, modelling clay, rolling pin, board, modelling tools, dark brown and red-brown paint, paintbrushes, kitchen paper, non-toxic varnish.

1 Cut off the top half of the plastic cup. Roll the piece of card into a tube shape. It should be wide enough for the bottom of the cup to sit into it neatly.

2 Overlap the edges of the rolled-up card. Glue or tape the edges to hold them in place. Fit the trimmed cup into the card tube, right side up.

3 Roll out the modelling clay. Cover the card tube with the clay. Use some of the clay to cover the plastic drinking cup, too. Leave the clay to dry.

PRIESTS

Brahmins wore a sacred white cotton cord across the chest. All boys of the Brahmin caste received the sacred cord at the age of about 11. It took nine years or more to learn a priest's duties. Brahmins were the only people allowed to teach the children of the three upper castes. People of these castes were known as 'twice-born' because they were accepted into adult life through a special ceremony. In one sacrificial hymn, the Brahmins are said to come from the mouth of the higher being, or Cosmic Man.

WARRIORS

The warrior noble, or Kshatriya, was the next highest caste after the Brahmin. The raja, who was the protector of society, came from the Kshatriya class. It was his duty to safeguard the position of each caste and to give money to the Brahmins. The Kshatriyas were thought to be the arms of the Cosmic Man.

ORDINARY PEOPLE

The Vaishyas were the common people of the Aryan clans. They were large in number and rich in wealth. They practised agriculture and trade, and were thought to be the 'thighs' of the Cosmic Man. They were above the peasants and people of no caste, who were considered 'impure'.

Offering cups were an important part of the ritual of the sacrifices that the Aryans made to the gods. The cups were always the same shape, and would have been filled with holy water.

4 Using a wooden modelling tool, carefully start to carve your chosen design into the modelling clay on the cup.

5 Finish carving the picture. Cut lines into the clay to add texture. This will help make your finished cup look as if it has been made from wood.

6 Paint the cup with dark brown paint. While it is still wet, wipe some of the paint off with kitchen paper, to give it a streaked look. Leave to dry.

7 Paint the cup with red-brown paint. The darker paint will still show through in places. Leave to dry, then brush the cup with two coats of varnish.

Buddhist India

THE CUSTOMS AND TEACHINGS of the Aryan people meant that the highest born Brahmins (priests) were the only ones who could be saved from life's suffering. People of other castes were not happy with this, and by 500BC new religious practices began to develop. Siddharta Gautama was born into the warrior caste, but left his family at the age of 30 to seek spiritual enlightenment (freedom). He gained many followers during his lifetime and became known simply as the Buddha, which means enlightened. He taught what he called a 'Middle Way' between pleasure and suffering, which everyone could follow regardless of caste.

The Buddha's followers evolved into an order of monks called the sangha, who wandered from place to place with a begging bowl and survived on people's donations. Many important people, including kings and merchants, gave generously to the sangha and built monasteries for them to live in. After the Buddha's death, his followers paid homage to him by building large domed monuments, called *stupas*.

From 272BC, King Ashoka encouraged the spread of Buddhism. Ashoka is said to have built an incredible 80,000 *stupas*, each with its own monastery.

RECORDED IN STONE
This relief from the AD500s shows events from Buddha's life. Scenes, such as his departure from his father's palace and his enlightenment under the bodhi tree, were recorded on monuments. There, they could be read by many people.

GIFTS TO THE BUDDHA
The *stupa* at Sanchi was built by Ashoka and added to by later monarchs. The dome is surrounded by a beautifully carved railing that shows scenes from the Buddha's life. At this *stupa* and several others at Sanchi, nearly 900 short inscriptions have been found. Each one records the gifts of monks and ordinary people.

CAVE MONASTERY
In western India, cave monasteries were built among the rocks to house communities of monks. Buddhist monks needed to be alone in order to meditate and follow the path to enlightenment.

ANCIENT AND MODERN
Modern monks in Sri Lanka worship an ancient statue of the Buddha. Buddhism was brought to Sri Lanka by Ashoka's son, Mahinda. The very oldest form of Buddhism, called Theravada, is still practised in Sri Lanka today.

PRAYER HANGING
A painting of the Buddha on a prayer hanging in the Tibet Autonomous Region (TAR) has a face that is more Central Asian than Indian. In the TAR, Buddhism grew into a new form called Vajrayana. This tradition often included secret teachings about rituals.

RELICS OF THE BUDDHA
A limestone carving at the great *stupa* in Nagarjunakonda, in eastern India, shows gods and men venerating (worshipping) the Buddha's relics. The relics are encased in the central mound of every *stupa*. Relics are pieces of bone or hair that Buddhists believe have come from the body of the Buddha.

Buddha's footprints

bodhi tree

SIGNS OF THE BUDDHA
Early Buddhist artists did not show the Buddha's body because they believed he had risen above existence. Instead, symbols of his life were shown. Footprints symbolized his presence yet absence. It was under the bodhi tree that Buddha achieved enlightenment.

Hindu Gods and Goddesses

BUDDHISM REMAINED the dominant religion in India until about AD200, but the religion of the Aryan people did not disappear. Instead, it evolved into new forms, which together became known as Hinduism. Many of the beliefs were the same, but Hinduism discouraged the Vedic practice of making animal sacrifices, and introduced new gods to replace the Aryan deities. Gradually, Hinduism took over from Buddhism, and has remained India's dominant religion ever since.

In the two main types of Hinduism – Vaishnavism and Shaivism – Hindus believe that one god (Vishnu or Shiva) rules the universe. From about AD1000, some worshipped the goddess Devi instead. In each version, the Cosmic Man (the god's representation on earth) takes on different forms depending on the task, so that Hindu mythology seems to have lots of gods. In fact, they are versions of Vishnu, Shiva or Devi.

TERRIBLE GOD
Shiva appears in the form of a terrifying being wielding a trident. At times, Shiva is associated with the destructive forces of the universe and commands demonic beings, called ganas.

HAPPY GOD
The conch shell and the discus are the symbols of the god Vishnu, who is often shown with blue skin. Vishnu mostly brings happiness, preservation and kingship. He stands on a lotus flower.

MAKE A GARLAND OF FLOWERS

You will need: Tissue paper in orange, yellow, red, pink and white, pencil, scissors, white glue, paintbrush, length of string, darning needle.

1 Draw simple flower shapes on to sheets of tissue paper. If you like, you can lay the sheets of paper in layers, one on top of the other.

2 Using scissors, cut out your flower shapes. Take care not to tear the tissue paper. Cut the same number of flowers in each shade of paper.

3 Scrunch up the tissue flower shapes with your hands. Then uncrumple them, but don't smooth them out too much.

GANESHA

The elephant god, Ganesha, is the son of Shiva. He is god of wisdom and prosperity and is known for his love of sweetmeats. Ganesha is always shown accompanied by a rat.

KRISHNA AND RADHA

The god Krishna was an incarnation of Vishnu on earth. Krishna was born as a cowherder. In his youth, he is said to have been adored by many women, but his preferred woman was Radha. The love of Radha and Krishna is the theme of many Hindu religious songs.

GODDESS OF DEATH AND WAR

Shiva's wife had many forms. The fiercest was Kali, goddess of death. Here, she holds an array of weapons in her many arms. Kings often worshipped Kali before going into battle.

Hindus make garlands of fresh flowers to wear at festivals to pay homage to their gods.

4 Glue the flower shapes together loosely in layers to make larger, single flowers. Use eight layers of tissue paper for each finished flower.

5 Now gently fluff up the layers of tissue paper with your fingers. This will make your flowers look much more impressive.

6 Measure a length of string that is long enough to go around your neck. Start to thread the flowers on to the string to make a garland.

7 Thread all the tissue flowers on to the length of string. When you have secured all the flowers, tie a double knot in the string to finish.

Epic Tales of the Gods

A Decisive Battle
Prince Arjuna and Krishna face the Kauravas on the battlefield. It is here that Krishna (painted blue) reveals that he is a god to Arjuna, and sings a song that instructs him on how to behave properly. Krishna's song is known as the *Bhagavad-Gita*.

Brothers in Arms
The five Pandava brothers are revered in this shrine. They are the heroes of the *Mahabharata* story. They struggle with the Kauravas to regain their kingdom, and are aided by Krishna. Each brother is known for a noble quality, such as heroism.

T HE MOST IMPORTANT ancient stories of the Hindus are told in two great epics (long poems) called the *Ramayana* and the *Mahabharata*. No one is sure exactly who wrote them or when, but they were written down in their present form by AD500. In both, the god Vishnu appears in different incarnations (forms) to save the earth from destruction and to tell people about right and wrong.

In the *Ramayana*, Vishnu takes the form of the exiled prince Rama. His wife, Sita, is abducted by the demon Ravana and taken to a fortress in Lanka (present-day Sri Lanka). Rama rescues Sita with the help of the monkey god, Hanuman.

The *Mahabharata* is a much longer story, with many subplots. It tells of a bitter struggle between two families, the Pandavas and the Kauravas. Krishna, another human version of Vishnu, helps the Pandavas to defeat the Kauravas. Part of the *Mahabharata* is Krishna's advice on morality to the Pandava prince, Arjuna. It is known as the *Bhagavad-Gita*, and is given just before the last battle, which the Pandavas finally manage to win.

Make a Ramayana Headdress
You will need: ruler, pencil, 2 x A2 sheet of thin red card, scissors, adhesive tape, strips of corrugated cardboard, red paint, paintbrushes, string, drawing pin, bright paints, white glue, bright foil wrappers.

1 Use a ruler and pencil to draw two straight lines at an angle as shown, onto card. Join these lines with curved lines, as shown, Cut out the shape.

2 Roll the card into a shape that is narrower at the top. The bottom of the card should be wide enough to fit your head. Fix the edges with tape.

3 Tape a strip of corrugated cardboard around the base of your headdress shape, but leave a gap at the back where the seam is.

RAMA ON THE ATTACK

With the help of Hanuman and his army of monkeys, and an army of bears, Rama attacks the forces of the demon Ravana in Lanka. Rama is victorious in his battle and kills Ravana. He is then reunited with his wife, Sita.

MONKEY KING

Hanuman, leader of the monkeys of the forest, became Rama's most faithful follower. As Rama searched desperately for his wife, Sita, it was Hanuman who found her in Ravana's palace in Lanka. Hanuman led Rama and his monkey forces to Sita's rescue.

THE DOOMED DEMON

Ravana, the demon king, leads his demon generals. In the *Ramayana*, Ravana was the all-powerful king of the island of Lanka. However, a prophecy foretold that he would lose his life because of a woman. That woman turned out to be Sita.

Hindus wear headdresses to act out scenes from the story of Rama and Sita.

4 Tape corrugated card strips around the middle and the top of your hat shape, again leaving a gap at the back. Paint the strips with red paint.

5 Measure the height of your headdress. Using string tied to a drawing pin and a pencil, draw a circle with a diameter that matches the height of your headdress.

6 Carefully cut out the circle. Now use bright paints and foil wrappers to decorate your headdress in bright patterns. Make the patterns as vivid as possible.

7 Leave the decorated circle to dry thoroughly. Then glue or tape it to the back of your headdress. Finally, decorate the headdress.

Houses of the Gods

A HINDU TEMPLE IS RATHER like a palace that has been built for a god to live in. In the old Aryan Vedic religion, people believed that the gods lived in the skies and were fed by the sacrificial fires. After each sacrifice, the altar was taken down. When Hinduism evolved, it adopted the Buddhist practice of building places of worship called *stupas*. Shaivas and Vaishnavas built beautiful temples and invited their gods to come and live in them in the form of images, such as statues. Brahmin priests looked after the statues, tending to their every need. The gods were woken, bathed, dressed, entertained and fed each day. This practice of revering a god's image is called *puja*, and is still central to Hinduism today.

By AD500, temples were common. As kings converted to Hinduism, they built many huge temples across India and lavished donations of money and tax revenue from farmlands upon them. By AD1000, most Hindu temples were not only places of worship but places where country people traded goods.

REVERING THE BUDDHA
This frieze is from a 2,000-year-old *stupa* at Amaravati, a Buddhist site in south India. It shows men and gods paying homage at the feet of the Buddha. Puja (worship) was first practised by Buddhists. It later became popular among Hindus as well.

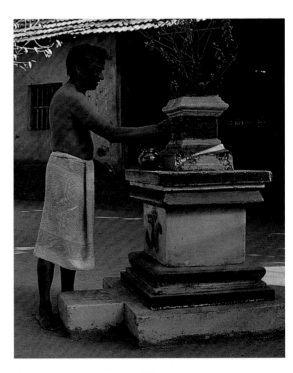

A SHRINE IN THE HOME
A man makes an offering at a shrine in his home. From early times, Hindus worshipped gods in the household, as well as in the temple. Most Hindus do not pray together, but privately, alone.

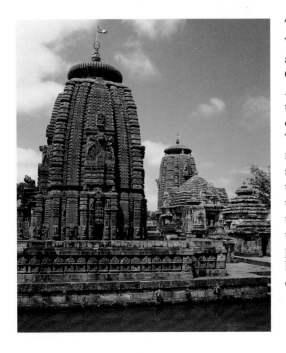

TEMPLE TOWER
The temple to Shiva at Bhubaneshwar in Orissa was built in the AD800s. The tower is the home of a *linga*, or symbol of Shiva. The tower itself is a mix of north and south Indian styles of temple. The central tower of another temple can be seen in the background of the picture. Kings often built several temples close to one another.

A PORTABLE SHRINE
This cloth was used as a portable shrine for worshipping the god Pabuji. Pabuji was a hero of the 1300s who was converted into a god. The pictures surrounding the figure of Pabuji represent scenes from his life as told in a folk story. Folk priests in the northern state of Rajasthan went from village to village carrying cloths like these, to use as temples.

SYMBOL OF POWER
A *gopuram* (gate tower) at the Shiva temple at the city of Madurai, in Tamil Nadu. *Gopuram* were built by kings as symbols of power, each king trying to outdo his rivals. This *gopuram* is so huge, it is larger than the shrine inside the temple itself. Gopurams are covered in painted carvings and can be seen from afar.

granite limestone sandstone

BUILDING MATERIALS
Hindu temples were made from local materials, such as limestone, granite and sandstone. After being quarried, the stone was usually cut into large blocks and then shaped. Temples were built without mortar to hold the blocks in place.

AT THE FEET OF THE SAINT
A worshipper performs *puja* (worship) to a saint in south India. His image is so huge that the priests can only reach his toes to place flower and coconut offerings. When the image is bathed, scaffolding is erected to reach the head.

The Coming of Islam

THE MUSLIM RELIGION, called Islam – which means submission to God – was founded in Arabia (present-day Saudi Arabia) by a man named Mohammed in AD622. It spread quickly into the countries around Arabia, but it took nearly 400 years for Islam to reach India.

In AD1007 Sultan Mahmud, the Muslim leader of the city of Ghazni in Afghanistan, started a series of attacks on northern India to loot the rich temples there. More Islamic leaders followed his example, and by AD1206, Muslim Turks from Central Asia had founded a new kingdom, or Sultanate, based in the city of Delhi. The Delhi Sultanate ruled the region for 300 years.

Islam gradually spread among ordinary people. Islamic sufis (mystics) played an important role in spreading the message of God's love for all people. They worshipped in a very emotional style at their countryside shrines, in a way that the Hindu peasants could understand. By the 1700s, nearly a quarter of India's population was Muslim. They showed great tolerance to other religions and cultures, especially the Hindu faith.

BEAUTIFUL WRITING
This page is from a Persian commentary on the holy book of Muslims, the *Quran*. Muslims were not allowed to represent images, such as humans, animals or flowers, in art. Instead they developed calligraphy (the art of beautiful writing).

SEAFARING SETTLERS
The Indian Ocean was in the power of Muslim traders from about AD700. They arrived along the south-western coast of India on their way to Indonesia and China, and were among the earliest Muslims to settle in India. These traders followed Muslim law. Different Muslim laws spread in India through further Muslim invasions from Turkey and Afghanistan in the 1100s and 1200s.

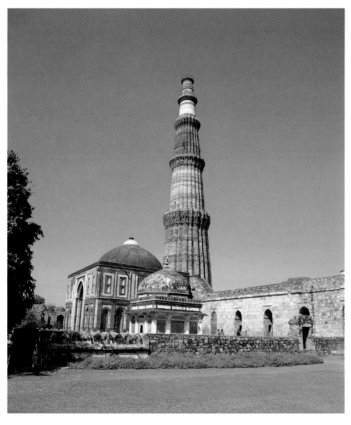

FROM TEMPLE TO MOSQUE
The Quwat al-Islam, a large mosque in Delhi, was built out of parts of destroyed temples of older faiths. It has two architectural features that were introduced to India by Islam. One feature is the arch, the other is the use of mortar for sticking bricks together. The mosque was built by the Delhi Sultanate in 1193.

HOLY MEN
Sufis (mystics) gather together to pray. Sufism was a type of Islam that preached that people's souls can communicate to God through ecstatic music, singing and dancing. Sufism came into prominence in Persia in the AD900s. By about 1100 it had also gained a foothold in the north-west of India.

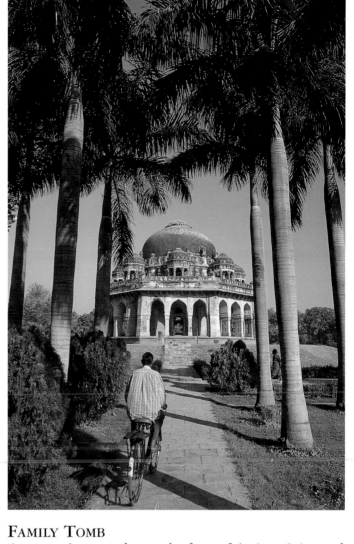

FAMILY TOMB
A man cycles towards a tomb of one of the later Sultans of Delhi. The tomb is in the gardens of the Lodi family, the last rulers of the Delhi Sultanate. The last Lodi Sultan was defeated in battle by the Mughal prince Babur, in 1526.

SUFI SHRINE
This tomb-shrine, or *dargah*, in Rajgir, reveres a famous sufi saint. Sufi teachers were called *pirs*, or *shaikhs*. They often had a large number of followers.

The Sikh Society

AS ISLAM SPREAD through northern India, Hinduism and Islam existed side by side. In the Punjab region of northern India, a new religion emerged that had elements of both. It was called Sikhism, and was founded by a man called Guru (teacher) Nanak (1469–1539). Sikhism rejected the strict Hindu caste system and adopted the Islamic idea that all people are equal before God, but kept many aspects of Hindu ritual. Sikhs worshipped in temples called gurdwaras (abode of the gurus). After Nanak, there were nine more gurus. The fifth, Arjan, founded the Golden Temple at Amritsar, which later became the holiest of all gurdwaras. He also wrote the Sikh holy book, or *Adi Granth*.

In the 1600s, the Muslim Mughal rulers in Delhi became concerned about the growth of this new religion. They began to persecute the Sikhs and killed Arjan and another guru. The tenth guru, Gobind Singh, decided that Sikhs should protect themselves and founded a military order called the khalsa. Members carried a comb and dagger, wore a steel bangle, breeches, and did not cut their hair. Sikh men took the title Singh (lion). After the death of Gobind Singh in 1708, there were no more gurus, but Sikhs continued to live by the teachings of the *Adi Granth.*

LETHAL TURBAN
A Sikh war turban is decorated with weapons that could be removed and used against the enemy during battle. Metal throwing rings could slice heads off, while 'claws' were for disembowelling people.

THE GOLDEN TEMPLE
The greatest Sikh temple is the Golden Temple in the Sikh holy city of Amritsar. The temple was built by Guru Arjan Singh (1581-1606). Its white marble walls and domes are decorated with gold. The city of Amritsar is named after the lake that surrounds the temple. Sikhs worship in their temples in large congregations (groups). Free kitchens are attached to Sikh temples, where all can eat.

SYMBOLIC COMB
This close-up picture of a Sikh turban shows the kangha, a comb that is pinned to the middle. The kangha is one of the five signs of the Sikh religion. Sikh men do not cut their hair – another sign of Sikhism.

THE SACRED BOOK
The *Adi Granth* is the sacred book of the Sikhs. Its text was compiled by Guru Arjan Singh in the late 1500s. After the death of the last teacher, Guru Gobind Singh, Sikhs came to accept these scriptures as the symbol of God. They took over the role of the teacher from the Gurus.

A MILITARY MAHARAJA
The Maharaja Ranjit Singh (1799–1838) holds court. The water tank of the Golden Temple can be seen in the background. Ranjit Singh led the Sikh army to victory against Afghan warlords and the collapsing Mughal Empire. He established a separate Sikh kingdom in the Punjab region of India.

AN ABLE WARRIOR
A Sikh soldier sits on a cushion in this portrait from the 1800s. When the British ruled India, they recruited many Sikhs into their army. Sikhs were regarded as one of India's most warlike peoples.

The Mughal Empire

I**N 1526, A PRINCE** from the area now called Uzbekistan invaded India from the north-west. His name was Babur. He swept across the country with a powerful army and soon arrived in Delhi, where he defeated the Sultanate and founded a new empire. His successors came to be known as the Mughals. The Mughal Empire was the last important dynasty of India before the British arrived in the 1700s.

Babur's grandson, Akbar, who ruled from 1556 to 1605, was a great Mughal leader. Although he was Muslim, he was tolerant of other religions and took Hindu princesses as his wives. Forty years later, the warlike Mughal ruler Aurangzeb returned to a stricter form of Islam and expanded the empire. The Mughals were patrons of the arts, and built glorious

palaces, gardens and tombs. Many of India's most precious works of art date from this era. Persian was the language of their court, but they also spoke Urdu, a mixture of Persian, Arabic and Hindi.

ORDERLY COURTIERS
Mughal nobles had to take part in court rituals. They had to arrive punctually at court, and line up in rows. Their dress and posture were very important. The cummerbund tied around the waist and the turban were signs of self-control. Courtiers guarded the palace strictly in turn.

THE FIRST MUGHAL EMPEROR
Babur defeats Ibrahim Lodi, the last sultan of Delhi, at the Battle of Panipat in 1526. Babur invaded India because he was unable to recapture his own homeland in Samarkand.

MAKE A LACQUERED STORAGE BOX

You will need: pencil, ruler, sheets of thin card, scissors, adhesive tape, newspaper, wallpaper paste or flour and water, bowl, fine sandpaper, bright and white paint in white, paintbrushes, non-toxic varnish.

1 Scale up the shape shown here to the size you want your box to be and copy the shape on to card. Cut out the shape and fix the edges with tape to form a box.

2 Draw four card triangles with sides the same length as the top of the box. Tape the triangles together to form a pyramid and cut off the top.

3 Add newspaper strips to the paste, or flour and water, to make papier mâché. Cover the box and lid with three layers of papier mâché. Dry between layers.

A POEM IN STONE

The emperor Shah Jahan commemorated his wife Mumtaz Mahal (who died in childbirth) by building this magnificent mausoleum. It was built between 1631 and 1648, and came to be known as the Taj Mahal. It is built of white marble from Rajasthan. The Taj Mahal is one of the most magnificent buildings in the world, and is the high point of Mughal art.

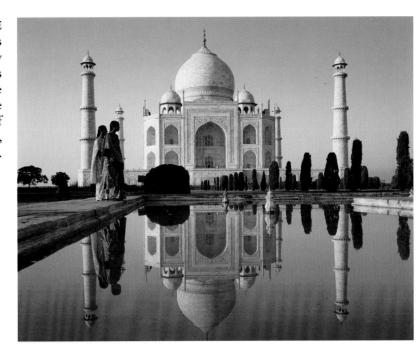

JADE HOOKAH

This Mughal period hookah (pipe) is made from precious green jade. During Mughal times, the culture of the court reached a high point in Indian history, with many fine pieces such as this being made.

RED PALACE

The Red Fort in Agra is one of the palaces built by Akbar. The Mughal emperors broke with the tradition of kings living in tents, and built sumptuous residences in their capital cities.

Lacquered boxes were popular with women of the royal court for storing adornments and jewels.

4 When the papier mâché is dry, smooth any rough edges with sandpaper. Add squares of cardboard as feet. Paint the box and the lid white.

5 Allow the painted box and lid to dry. Draw a pattern on to the box and lid. You could copy the pattern shown here, or use your own design.

6 Paint the lid and the box, including the feet, with bright paints. Use the pattern that you have drawn as a guide. Leave to dry.

7 To finish, paint the box and lid with a coat of non-toxic varnish. Leave to dry completely, then add a final coat of varnish. Your storage box is now finished.

The Symbols of Royalty

Over the centuries, kings of many different religions ruled India. The titles that they took and the objects that surrounded them often had symbolic significance and tell us a lot about their role as leaders. From the time of Ashoka, around 250BC, the ruler of the empire was called *cakravartin* (wheel-turner). The wheel was a Buddhist symbol for the world, so this suggested that the king made the world go round. Objects that were symbols of royalty included sceptres, crowns and yak-tail fly whisks. The most important object was the *chatra* (umbrella), which signified the king's protection of his realm.

Later, Hindu kings (called maharajadhirajas) developed the idea that the god Vishnu lived within them. When Islam arrived, the sultans showed their obedience to the *caliph*, the head of Islam in Baghdad, by taking titles such as *nasir* (helper). Mughals took Persian titles such as *padshah*, which simply means emperor.

DISPLAY OF POWER
A Mughal emperor rides through the city on top of an elephant, a symbol of royalty. Kings often processed through their cities to display their power and majesty. They were always followed by attendants and courtiers.

THE MARKS OF A KING
A picture of the man/god Rama's foot depicts the lotus, conch shell, umbrella, fly whisk and other royal symbols. People thought that a world-ruling king was born with special features. Among these were unique marks on the soles of his feet and palms of his hands, which foretold that he would be emperor.

MAKE A *CHAURI*
You will need: 3 x 25cm/1 x 10in strip corrugated cardboard, raffia, scissors, adhesive tape, white glue, 20cm/8in length of dowel, self-hardening modelling clay, paint in gold and a contrasting tone, paintbrushes, foil wrappers.

1 Put the strip of card on a covered, flat surface. Cut strips of raffia. Carefully tape the strands of raffia to the card. Leave your *chauri* to dry.

2 Wrap the card and raffia around the dowel, and glue it in place. Keep the card 2cm/¾in from the top, so that the dowel supports the raffia.

3 Tape the card and raffia band firmly in place to make sure that it will not come undone when you use your whisk. Leave the whisk to dry.

A KING'S HALO

The king in this procession has a halo surrounding his head. From Mughal times, rulers were thought to be blessed with the divine light of wisdom. This was represented in pictures by a halo.

ROYAL CUSHION

Raja Ram Singh of Jodhpur sits with his nobles. Only the king may sit on a cushion. The Rajputs were the kings of northern India, who fought against Muslim invaders but later became their most important military allies under the Mughals.

ROYAL RAMA

Rama, the human form of the god Vishnu, sits with his wife Sita and his brothers. He holds a bow, a symbol of courage. Also seen are other symbols of royalty – an umbrella and a yak-tail whisk.

The fly whisk was a symbol of a Hindu king's power.

4 Make lots of small beads from clay. Glue these on to the dowel in a circle, about 2.5cm/1in below the strip of card. Leave to dry.

5 Paint the dowel and beads with two coats of gold paint. Leave it to dry. Then paint a pattern on the strip of card and the dowel, in different shades.

6 When the paint is dry, glue bits of foil to your *chauri*. The more decorations you add, the more it will look like a real *chauri*.

Entertainments

THE ROYAL COURTS of Mughal India were places of wonderful entertainment. Courtiers listened to poetry and music every day. They loved riddles and word games, and in contests, poets were given half a verse and asked to complete it. Different art forms were connected to one another. For example, the *Natyashastra*, an ancient text on dance and drama, includes a long section on music. Dancers were also storytellers, using hand gestures to show meaning.

North and south India developed their own musical traditions – Hindustani in the north and Karnatak in the south. Islam introduced new instruments, such as the *sitar* (a stringed instrument) and the *tabla* (a drum). Outside the courts, religion played a part in the development of singing. Muslim mystics sang and played musical pieces called *qawwali*, while Hindus sang songs to Krishna.

JOYFUL OCCASION
Drummers and trumpeters at the Mughal court joyfully proclaim the birth of Akbar's son, Prince Salim. Music was often used to announce celebrations. Though they enjoyed royal patronage and were often renowned for their talent, musicians, dancers and actors were generally considered to be of low social standing.

INSTRUMENTAL BIRD
An instrument called a *sarangi* has been finely carved in the shape of a peacock. The *sarangi* was played with a bow and usually accompanied the dance performances of courtesans during late Mughal times.

MAKE A PAIR OF ANKLETS

You will need: measuring tape, gardening wire, pliers, strips of red felt fabric, scissors, glue or adhesive tape, darning needle, strong thread, silver bells.

1 Measure the diameter of your ankle. Multiply this figure by three, then add 4cm/1½in for a loop. Use the pliers to cut two pieces of wire to this length.

2 Loop the first cut piece of wire around itself about three times. Twist it tightly as you go. Then twist the second piece of wire in the same way.

3 Using the pliers, bend one end of each strip of twisted wire to form a loop. Bend the other end to form a hook. These act as a fastener.

FOLK DANCING

A decorative border shows figures linking hands in a Punjabi folk dance. Ordinary village people danced to celebrate births, weddings and many other special occasions. Each dance usually involved lots of dancers.

ON A STRING

A woman from Rajasthan plays with a yo-yo. Games with balls and strings were not expensive, so they could be enjoyed by both rich and poor people. Many other kinds of games were afforded only by the wealthy.

ENTERTAINING AT COURT

Dancers perform the style of dance known as a Kathak for the great Mughal emperor Akbar. Dance was a popular form of entertainment at court. Many of the complicated dance styles known in India today originated at the courts of kings in ancient times. The dances performed at court often told a story.

Anklets were worn by dancers who performed at ceremonies in the royal courts of the Mughals.

4 Cut out two strips of felt fabric that are slightly longer than your strips of wire. Glue or tape a felt strip on to the end of the twisted wire.

5 Wrap the felt around the wire, overlapping the edges of the felt. Glue the end of the felt to the place where you began. Wrap the second wire strip.

6 Thread a darning needle with sewing thread. Sew lots of tiny silver bells to the felt fabric covering your wire loops.

7 Repeat your stitches several times to make sure that the bells stay firmly in place. Add more bells, so that you cover both anklets completely.

Games and Sports

IMPORTANT PIECES
Sandstone and terracotta dice and other game pieces were discovered in the Indus valley. We cannot be certain what games these dice were used for. However, later Indian literature has recorded the importance of dice in playing games.

MANY GAMES DEVELOPED in the royal courts, where people had leisure time on their hands. One of these games, called *caturanga*, developed into the modern game of chess. *Caturanga* referred to the four parts of the army – the infantry, chariots, cavalry and elephants. It had different rules from modern chess, though it is not known exactly what these rules were. The game was played with dice, and up to four players may have taken part at once.

Outdoor sports were usually associated with *shikar* (hunting), and included archery, falconry (hunting with birds of prey) and horsemanship. Muslim rulers brought the game of polo, played on horseback, from Persia.

Religious fairs and festivals gave ordinary people the chance to play games, too. Cockfighting, ramfighting and wrestling were important. Spring was the season of playfulness. The ancient spring festival, Holi, is associated with love and play, and people had great fun throwing dyed powders and water over each other. Social roles were relaxed during the games of Holi, and people from different castes mixed freely. Holi is still celebrated today.

BOARD GAME
Archaeologists have found board games, such as the one pictured above, and toy animals in the Indus valley. These show that the Indus people must have enjoyed playing with toys and games.

A DANGEROUS SPORT
Wrestling was a favourite sport as long ago as 1000BC, and many kings had the title *malla* (wrestler). Wrestlers endured strict diets and physical training in camps known as *akharas*. Wrestling could be a highly dangerous activity. One inscription tells of a wrestler who was accidentally killed during a match.

PLAYING AT WARFARE
Mughal nobles play a game of polo. First played in Persia, polo was introduced to India by Muslim conquerors in the 1200s. The game was originally intended to train cavalry (soldiers on horseback) as it developed good horse-handling skills and taught riders how to ride and adjust their course at close quarters. Under the Mughals, polo became a popular sport among the nobility. However, it has never lost its military associations, and the Indian army maintains a polo team to this day.

DEER HUNTER
A Mughal king hunts deer. Hunting was an important activity. Like battle, it was an occasion to display the manhood of the king. The preferred prey were lions, tigers, boars and deer. In Mughal times, the emperor would hold secret meetings, and put his closest servants to the test during the hunt.

FLYING A KITE
A Mughal woman flies a kite. Kite-flying was a favourite sport in Mughal times. Competitions were so fierce that kite-fliers would dip the strings of their kites in crushed glass in order to cut down rival kites from the sky.

A GAME OF STRATEGY
A Mughal period chess set of painted ivory from Rajasthan. Chess was used to educate princes, ministers and nobles at court, and sharpen their planning skills. The most important chess board piece – the king – has the least power, as he acts through those around him. This was similar to how Indians viewed their own king.

The Importance of Animals

ANIMALS WERE PART OF everyday life throughout Indian history. Cows, oxen, water buffaloes, camels, horses and elephants carried loads, were used for transport and helped with farming. Hindus came to see the cow as the source of all life, and therefore the most important animal of all. It became protected and holy, and to this day Hindus are forbidden to harm them.

People kept pets as well, especially birds. They had peacocks in their gardens, and caged parrots, which were often taught how to speak. Muslim nobles also kept pigeons.

Animals played an important part in Hindu myths. For example, the god Vishnu incarnated himself as a turtle and a boar to save the world. Shiva's son Ganesha had an elephant's head, and the man god Rama's most faithful companion was Hanuman, king of the forest monkeys. In the *Pancatantra* fables, each animal symbolized a human virtue or vice. Lions, tigers and elephants were considered powerful, noble, brave and proud, but dogs were seen as unclean creatures with no self-respect. Jackals and herons were greedy and cunning, while the monkey was playful and foolish.

SYMBOL OF ROYALTY
Lions became the most common symbol of courage and nobility in India. They feature on this Ashokan pillar dating from around 250BC. This pillar was adopted as the symbol of the Indian republic in 1948.

MYTHICAL MAKARA
The makara is one of the mythical animals of India. It was a cross between an alligator and a tortoise. Makaras were a much-loved of artists and appear frequently as decorations on *stupas* and temples.

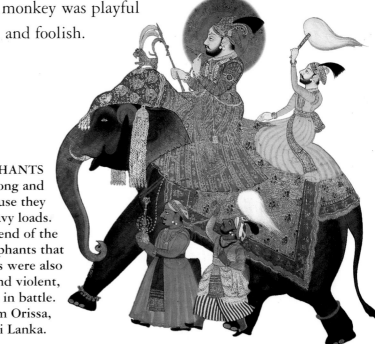

MIGHTY ELEPHANTS
Elephants were seen as strong and supporting, no doubt because they were often used to carry heavy loads. It was believed that at the end of the earth were heavenly elephants that held up the sky. Elephants were also thought to be fierce and violent, and were chosen for use in battle. The best elephants were from Orissa, in eastern India, and from Sri Lanka.

CHARMING THE SNAKES
A snake charmer coaxes a cobra from a basket to amuse the Hindu god Shiva. Snake charmers were known for their ability to lure and mesmerize snakes. They did this, not through the noise of their flute, but by using the movement of their hands and body to hold the reptile's attention. Snake charmers are still popular in India today.

CAT AND MOUSE
A cat sits inside a palace, while a mouse escapes across the roof. Cats were not usually treated as pets, but were tolerated as part of the household because they played an important role in controlling vermin, such as rats.

parrot

TALKATIVE PARROTS
Parrots and other talking birds were kept by wealthy people in cities in India. The birds were trained to speak by the people of the court. Since medieval times, many stories tell of parrots who blurted out the secrets of the palace in front of visitors!

BEAUTIFUL GUARDIANS
Peacocks were kept in gardens to help ward off snakes and to add to the beauty of the surroundings. They were also exported to the courts of emperors in Rome, China and Persia as exotic gifts. The peacock's brilliant plumage inspired the design of many textile patterns in India.

Writing and Language

THE EARLIEST KNOWN WRITING IN INDIA has been found on some seals from the ancient civilization of the Indus valley, but no one has yet been able to work out what the symbols mean. Later, when the Aryan people arrived, they brought a language with them that then developed into a number of different regional languages. There was one formal version of all these, which was called Sanskrit.

In about 300BC, a new form of script (writing) appeared, called Brahmi. The Buddhist king Ashoka used this script to inscribe proclamations on rocks and pillars all over his empire, and by about 100BC, Brahmi was used throughout India.

Early Indian documents were written on sheaves of palm leaf or bark, which were then threaded together. Important documents, which needed to last for a long time, were engraved on copper plates. The coming of Islam brought the Persian language to India, along with Arabic writing, which was developed into an art form called calligraphy. By Mughal times, paper and ink were replacing older methods of record keeping.

A WOODEN INSCRIPTION
This wooden tablet contains a Buddhist text written in a script known as Kharosthi. It was the script of a group of people who lived in north-west India from the first to the third centuries AD. The kings who ruled them wanted their people to follow Buddhism.

CARVED IN STONE
A stone inscription of AD900 on the pedestal of a Buddhist image from eastern India is written in Sanskrit. The image was given by a Buddhist monk for the benefit of his parents and teacher. The inscription is in an eastern form of *nagari*, the script used for modern Hindi.

MAKE A SUTRA
You will need: two 30 x 9cm/12 x 3½in pieces of balsa wood or cardboard, dark brown paint, paintbrushes, clear non-toxic varnish, A2 sheet of white paper, cold tea, scissors, ruler, pencil or bradawl, large darning needle, string or twine.

1 Brush the two 30 x 9cm/12 x 3½in rectangular pieces of balsa wood or card with brown paint so that they look like dark wood. Leave to dry.

2 Varnish your painted book covers. Leave them to dry. Give them a second coat, and a third. The extra coats will give the book a laquered finish.

3 Scrunch up the sheet of paper so that it wrinkles. Unscrunch it, lay it out flat and paint it with cold tea. Leave it to dry. This makes it look old.

MUGHAL PAINTER AND SCRIBE

A young painter from the Mughal court, named Manohar, sits with the scribe Mohammad Husain al-Kashmiri surrounded by inkwell, pen box, books and letters. They are writing in Persian, the language of the Mughal court and administration.

A MUGHAL WRITING SET

A jewel-inlaid box dating from Mughal times contains writing materials. These include a letter opener, a pen, a spoon and an in-built inkwell.

INSCRIBED TOWER

An extract from the *Quran*, the Muslim holy book, decorates the Qutb Minar, a 72m/235ft-high tower in Delhi. The tower was built in the AD1200s by Qutb-ud-Din Aibak, the first Muslim sultan of Dehli, to celebrate his victory over the Hindu kings. The art of beautiful writing, or calligraphy, was highly developed in Islamic cultures.

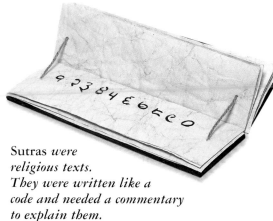

Sutras *were religious texts. They were written like a code and needed a commentary to explain them.*

4 When it is completely dry, cut the crinkled paper into rectangular pieces measuring 29 x 8cm/ 11½ x 3in. These will be the pages of your book.

5 Mark a point in the middle of each book cover, about 2cm/¾in from each short edge. Use a pencil or bradawl to make holes in the book covers.

6 Put the paper pages between the two book covers. Use a large needle to thread string or twine through the paper and the book covers.

7 Knot the ends of the string or twine firmly. Make sure that the knot is bigger than the hole in the book cover, so that the pages stay in place.

Homes of Rich and Poor

HOUSES IN INDIA differed according to social class. Poor people made their homes out of mud, clay and thatch. Materials such as these do not last long, so few of these houses have survived. By about 600BC, wealthier people were building homes made of brick and stone. It is thought that people's caste determined not only the part of a town or city that they lived in, but also what colour they painted their homes. The Brahmins of Jodhpur in Rajasthan, for example, painted their houses blue.

A wealthy man's house of about AD400 had a courtyard and an outer room where guests were entertained. Behind this were the inner rooms where the women of the house stayed and where food was cooked. Beyond the house itself there were often gardens and fountains surrounded by an outside wall. Homes like this stayed much the same in design over many centuries.

Royal palaces were more elaborate. They had many courtyards and enclosures surrounded by numerous walls. These were to protect the king from beggars and servants who might make a nuisance of themselves. Unlike ordinary homes, palaces changed in design with each new wave of rulers.

DECORATED DOORSTEP
Pictures in chalk and rice powder were drawn on the doorsteps of houses. Over time, they came to signify prosperity and good luck. Making such drawings was one of 64 forms of art that a cultured person was expected to be able to do.

birdcage

mango leaves hung for good luck

water trough

courtyard

MOUNTAIN HOMES
These modern mountain homes made from mud and thatch continue a tradition that is thousands of years old. Unlike valley homes, they have to be well insulated for protection against the colder climate.

THE GOOD LIFE
Life in a rich man's household was divided between the inner area, where he slept and ate, and the outer regions, dominated by a courtyard where he entertained friends, read, listened to music and strolled in the garden. Here, salons (groups) of men would meet to discuss life and politics.

wooden eaves

outer room for
entertaining

clay walls

chimney to
vent smoke

terracotta tiles

kitchen area

hearth for cooking

pressed dirt or
clay floor

rubble-filled
walls with
plaster covering

FANCY CANOPY
The highly decorated ceiling
of a room in a merchant's
fortified home. These
houses, called *havelis*, were
built by Rajput kings and
rich merchants of Rajasthan.

limes

mango
leaves

rice flour

GOOD LUCK CHARMS
Various foods and plants were placed
at the entrance of a household for
good luck. These included rice-flour
drawings on the step, and mango
leaves and limes – which were usually
hung above the door frame.

A Woman's Place

ORDINARY WOMEN did not have an easy life in India. They toiled in the fields and threshed the wheat. In some parts of India and among Muslims, women had to dress very modestly and some were not allowed to go out at all. Women from rich families were symbols of a man's wealth. The more wives he had the better, as it showed that he was rich enough to look after them. Kings had several wives, too, because marrying women from different regions was a way of forming alliances. Very occasionally, queens became leaders. Queen Raziya, for example, was sultan in the 1200s.

For nearly 2,000 years in Indian art and literature, women ideally have had long hair, almond-shaped eyes, a sweet birdlike voice and a shy manner. Sometimes they were portrayed as romantic heroines, such as Rama's virtuous wife Sita in the *Ramayana*. Hinduism also had many goddesses. Saraswati was the goddess of learning, Lakshmi the goddess of wealth and Durga the goddess of warfare.

IDEAL BEAUTY
This woman is shown with large, almond-shaped eyes – the ideal of beauty in ancient India. Women lined their eyes with a black paste called collyrium, to accentuate the almond shape.

QUEST FOR KNOWLEDGE
Female Hindu ascetics (who practise self-denial) surround their leader in a holy hermitage. Rarely could women abandon worldly life for spiritual pursuits, as men did. Usually, only widows were allowed to take the spiritual path.

TIE A SARI

You will need: silky or cotton fabric measuring 4 x 1m/4 ½yds x 40in, large safety pin. To make a decorated border, dip a cork into gold paint and print a pattern along one long edge of the fabric. Leave to dry.

1 Hold one corner of the fabric to your stomach with the decorated border on the outside. Wrap the long side of the fabric once around your waist.

2 Make a number of pleats where the fabric comes back to the front again. Make them as even as you can. The pleats act as the sari's underskirt.

3 Tuck the pleated section into the waist of the underskirt. You could hold the pleats in place with safety pins, while you practise tying the sari.

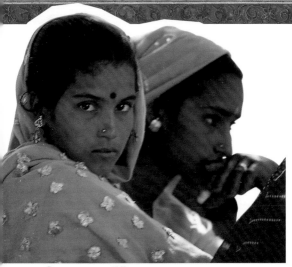

COVERED HAIR

These women from Rajasthan cover their hair with their saris. The spread of Islam influenced the habits of Hindu women in northern India. They had to dress according to what was considered modest by Muslims.

MORE THAN ONE WIFE

Mughal emperor Shah Jahan is shown with one of his wives, Qudsia Begum. Both Hindu and Muslim men of rank often took more than one wife. Though this increased the chance of producing heirs, it could also create jealousy within the royal household.

HARD DAY'S WORK

Female workers pick tea in north-eastern India. Though tea was not drunk in India, women worked in the fields to cultivate other crops. Low-caste peasant women formed the most exploited class in society.

A sari is a single large cloth covering both the upper and lower body. Saris were first worn in eastern India over a 1,000 years ago.

FOOD FOR THE FAMILY

A woman prepares food for her family. Women of the working classes have had a hard life throughout India's history. They not only worked in the fields, but were responsible for most household work, too.

4 Take the excess length of fabric in your left hand and pass it all the way around your back. Take care that the pleats don't come out.

5 Now take the rest of the fabric in your right hand and lift it up so that it is level with your shoulders. Do this in front of a mirror, if possible.

6 Swing the fabric over your left shoulder. The fabric should fall in gentle folds from your shoulder, across your body, to your waist.

7 Carefully pin the fabric to the shoulder of your tee-shirt, to keep it in place. Look in a mirror, to see if it fits well. If it doesn't, try again!

Village India

A VILLAGE HOME
Cane houses with thatched roofs have been typical of villages in eastern India for hundreds of years. The stone foundation raises the floor of this house above light flooding levels. Other building materials for village structures include mud, clay and wood.

Throughout history, most people in India have lived in the country rather than in towns, so village life has always been an essential part of Indian civilization. This worked in one of two ways. Some villages were tribal, which meant that the villagers organized their own lives and were independent from other rulers. In other villages, the people were peasants, which meant that they were controlled by local rulers or emperors, and had to pay taxes.

From medieval times onwards, more and more villagers became peasants. Whether they were peasants or tribal, however, people had plenty of contact with towns and cities, because they provided city-dwellers with food. The taxes demanded by rulers were often in the form of food, too.

Villagers farmed differently depending upon where they lived. In drier and higher regions it was difficult to grow crops. Villagers in these areas grew a few crops and kept animals. They often remained tribal. In the fertile plains and river basins, rice cultivation supported densely populated and complex societies, which grew into great empires.

A CRUCIAL CROP
Terraced paddy fields in the hills of eastern India have been flooded with water. Rice cultivation requires elaborate irrigation techniques, as the plant's root must be submerged in water. Rice cultivation was the dominant agricultural activity in central, eastern and southern India in the past, as now. Rice was a high-yield crop, and it could feed large numbers of people. This in turn gave rise to advanced societies and massive empires.

BULLOCK CART
A villager and his bullock arrive at the construction site of a Mughal palace. Bullock carts were the most common vehicles in villages. They carried heavy loads of grain and rice, and building materials, too.

WASHING CLOTHES
A village *dhobi* (washerman) cleans clothes in a river. He scrubs the clothes on stone slabs beside the river. Behind the *dhobi*, men are working on a building site.

THE MARKET
A Mughal period painting shows food being sold at a village market. Milk is being drawn from a cow, and rice and water are being sold. Each village or cluster of villages had a street market where produce was bought and sold.

barley

lentils

basmati rice

STAPLE FOODS
Rice, barley and lentils were the most common foods grown in rural villages. Dishes that used these ingredients formed the people's main diet. As the village poor could generally not afford meat, lentils were an important source of protein.

TYPICAL VILLAGE LIFE
A caravan (a group of merchants travelling together) passes by a river near Murshidabad with three villages nearby. Villagers bathe by the river and plough the fields. Horses and camels can be seen in a horse market. In the foreground an ascetic receives visitors.

Money and Trade

TRADE WITH DISTANT COUNTRIES has been important for India as far back as the ancient civilization of the Indus Valley. Later, trade routes became established up and down the length of India as well as with faraway places. Luxurious and precious goods such as spices, jewels, ebony, ivory and teak, were the main trade objects.

One highly prized import was silk from China.

The first coins in India, which had very simple designs, date from about 500BC. They were probably introduced from Persia (modern Iran).

By about 100BC, coins were widely used to pay for goods and services in city markets and courts, but were less common in villages, where people simply exchanged goods, a practice called bartering. Bartering remained the normal way of trading for villagers until Mughal times.

Many different types of coins were produced, including square ones. Some had portraits of kings and gods on them, and were often inscribed with the name of the ruling king. They were made of gold, silver, copper and alloys (mixes of metals). Silver seems to have been frequently used for the best coins, but it sometimes ran short when it was in demand for making statues and ornaments instead.

HEADS OR TAILS
A king of the Gupta dynasty with a stringed instrument is shown on a gold coin dating from around AD350. Portraits of ancient Hindu royalty were most often to be found on coins. Few other likenesses, such as sculptures or carvings, exist of ancient Hindu kings.

SHELLING OUT
Cowrie shells were used as currency (money) in coastal areas. They were also used inland when precious metals were scarce. Cowries were the lowest form of coinage. In one court poem, it is said that King Ramapala of Bengal paid his army in cowrie shells.

TRADE ROAD FOR SILK
The Silk Road stretched for more than 7,000km/4,500 miles from China to Anatolia (modern Turkey) and beyond. It was a trade route for items such as silk, jewels and spices. Voyagers along the Silk Road also brought new ideas. China and Central Asia were introduced to Buddhism, and many Chinese pilgrims came to India via the Silk Road.

saffron

TRADING IN SPICE

Saffron is an aromatic spice grown in north India. Sandalwood is a musky-smelling wood, produced mainly in the south. Both were rare and valuable, and were among India's most prized trading items. They were exported to the Middle East and to China.

ARAB TRADING VESSEL

This painting shows an Arab trading ship. The Indian Ocean became an important trading zone after the rise of Islam in the AD600s. The ocean linked the powerful empires of Arabia to eastern lands, including India, South-east Asia and China. Muslim merchants ruled the seas from the AD700s until the coming of the Europeans in the 1500s.

TRADERS JOURNEYING TOGETHER

A wall mural from Rajasthan shows a caravan (a group of merchants travelling together). Camels were ideal for travel in western Rajasthan, which is mostly desert. From Mughal times, Rajasthani merchants were famous throughout India for being good at making money,

COIN MEDALLION

A gold coin of the Mughal emperor Jahangir (1605-1627) has a portrait on one side and a Persian inscription on the other. This coin was probably not used in trade but was instead worn as a sign of the emperor's esteem. Using coins as decorations – especially if the coins were made of gold – dates back to the AD100s. At that time Roman coins were made into adornments in southern India.

Dress and Accessories

CLOTHING HAS ALWAYS BEEN quite simple in India. Noble people, both men and women, usually wore a single piece of fabric that was draped around the hips, drawn up between the legs, then fastened securely again at the waist. Women wore bodices above the waist, but men were often barechested. Although their clothes were simple, people had elaborate hairstyles that included flowers and other decorations. Men and women also wore a lot of adornments, such as earrings, armbands, breastplates, noserings and anklets. The Hindu male garment was called the *dhoti*, and the female garment gradually evolved into the sari – a single large cloth draped around the body, with a bodice worn underneath.

When Islam arrived, tailored garments became widespread in northern India. People wore sewn cotton trousers called *paijama* or *shalwar*, with a long tunic called a *kamiz* or *kurta*. For men, turbans became popular. Muslim women were expected to dress modestly, so they began to wear veils, a practice that Hindu women also adopted.

SETTING THE TREND
Bangles and ear studs from the Indus Valley are among the earliest ornaments found in India. They are more than 4,000 years old. The styles of these adornments, and the designs on them, were used again in later forms of decoration.

ANCIENT BEAUTY AIDS
This mirror, collyrium applicator and hair pin are over 4,000 years old. Large dark eyes were considered a sign of beauty, so women drew attention to their eyes by outlining them with collyrium, a black substance.

ANCIENT DRESS
A painted fragment of a pillar shows a woman wearing a long red skirt and adornments. The pillar is about 2,000 years old.

MAKE A FLOWER BRACELET

You will need: A5 sheets of thin white card, pencil, scissors, gold paint, paintbrush, A5 sheets of white paper, white glue, foil papers, gardening wire, pliers.

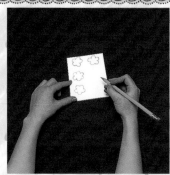

1 Draw some simple flower shapes on the white card. They should be about 2cm/¾in in diameter. Give each flower six rounded petals.

2 Carefully cut out each of the flower shapes. Then paint both sides of each flower with gold paint. Leave the flowers to dry.

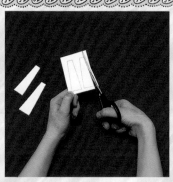

3 Draw 10 to 12 wedge shapes on the white paper sheets. They should be wider at the bottom than at the top. Cut out the wedge shapes.

HINDU DRESS

In this detail from a painted panel, a Hindu man and woman wear typical dress – a *dhoti* for the man and for the woman, a sari. Both men and women liked to wear bright clothes.

silk

VIVID SILK

Silk is a fine, soft thread produced by the larva (grubs) of the silkworm moth when it makes its cocoon. The thread is woven into cloth and dyed. Silk was first brought to India from China along the Silk Road. Indian silk is mostly dyed in bright hues.

JEWELS FOR ALL

A Rajasthani woman wears traditional adornments and dress. Nowadays in India, ornaments are still so valued that even the poorer peasants own pieces for special occasions.

Floral designs are common patterns used throughout Indian art.

CLOTHING FOR THE COURT

Courtiers from Mughal times wear a side-fastening coat called a *jama*. It has a tight body, high waist and flared skirt reaching to below the knees. It is worn over tight-fitting trousers, or *paijama*, gathered at the ankle. A sash, called a *patuka*, is tied at the waist. Courtiers also wore a small turban as a mark of respect.

4 Apply glue to the wedge shapes and roll them up to make beads, leaving a hole through the middle. Paint the beads gold and leave to dry.

5 Carefully cut out tiny circles from the foil wrappers. Make sure you have enough to stick on to the middle of each flower.

6 Measure gardening wire long enough to go around your wrist. Add 4cm/1½in for a loop. Tape the flowers to the wire and thread on the beads.

7 To finish the flower bracelet, use a pair of pliers to bend back one end of the wire to form a loop and the other end to form a hook.

Textiles and Printing

MAKING TEXTILES HAS ALWAYS BEEN an important activity in India. There are records of ancient Romans buying Indian cloth, so the textile trade must have been well established by then. As fabric does not last very well, there are few examples from before AD900, but sculptures show us the kinds of cotton cloth that were made. In Buddhist and Hindu sculptures, clothing is generally light and draws attention to the shape of the body.

India's textiles show a lot of different influences. Silk originally came from China, but from about AD100 it was produced in India and became an important Indian export. From about AD1100, Turkish and then Persian invaders introduced floral designs. Fine carpets also began to be made following Persian traditions and styles. Some places began to specialize in the production or sale of textiles. In Mughal times, silks and muslin (fine cotton fabric) were produced at Ahmedabad, Surat and Dhaka, while Kanchipuram, near Madras, became known for its fine silk saris. The Coromandel coast, Gujarat and Bengal all became textile export centres.

DRAPED GARMENT
A red sandstone figure from Jamalpur dates from about AD400, and shows the Buddha dressed in a fine muslin (cheesecloth) garment. Many clothes in ancient India were draped and folded rather than sewn.

SPINNING WHEEL
A woman sits at her spinning wheel. Weavers were important because Indian fabrics were in great demand in Europe.

MAKE A PRINTING BLOCK

You will need: paper, felt-tipped pen, scissors, halved raw potato, blunt knife, 20 x 15cm/8 x 6in piece of beige calico fabric, iron, scrap paper, paints, paintbrush.

1 Copy the pattern shown here on to a sheet of paper. You can invent your own Indian design, if you prefer. Carefully cut out the pattern.

2 Place the cut-out pattern on the cut surface of the halved potato. Draw around the outline of the pattern with a felt-tipped pen.

3 Use the knife to cut away the potato around the pattern. Your pattern should be raised about 5mm/¼in above the rest of the potato half.

PERSIAN-STYLE CARPET

This fine, wool carpet is decorated with floral patterns. In Mughal times, many fine carpets like this one were produced in India. Carpet weaving was a skill learned in the north-west of India from Persian craftworkers.

indigo block   *madder*

RED AND BLUE DYES

Dark-red dye made from the root of the madder plant, and violet-blue dye made from the leaves of the indigo plant were used to dye textiles during Mughal times. Little is known about the way in which textiles were dyed in earlier times.

PRINTING COTTON CLOTH

A Punjabi man prints a pattern on to a length of cotton with a printing block. Dyes for cotton cloth were usually made from vegetables.

HUNTING COAT

This satin hunting coat has scenes and animals of the hunt embroidered on it in silk. It is typical of the type of dress worn by Mughal nobles.

Printing blocks were used in Mughal times to decorate fabric for festivals and other special occasions.

4 Ask an adult to help you to iron the fabric. Lay the ironed fabric on top of scrap paper. Apply paint to part of your printing block with a paintbrush.

5 Brush a different shade of paint on to your printing block. Give the block an even coat of paint that is not too heavy. Do not drench the block.

6 Press the printing block on to the fabric a few times. When the paint design starts to fade, apply more paint to the block with the paintbrush.

7 When the print design has dried, add some bright details. Try out different paints on your printing block, or alter the pattern on the fabric.

49

Gardens

THE GARDENS of the Mughals were enclosed spaces filled with pools and flowering plants. As they required constant care and watering, gardens were only for wealthy people who could afford staff. Gardeners worked hard to ensure that parts of the garden were in bloom all year round. Courtiers amused themselves in gardens by playing games such as hide-and-seek, or with cockfighting. For at least 2,000 years, Indians have been especially fond of flowers. The mango blossom, ashoka flower and jasmine all appeared in courtly poetry. The lotus (a kind of water-lily), with its underwater stem system and floating flower, was a symbol of goodness and life. Flowers and leaves were used to make garlands to decorate the body and hair, and to decorate images of Hindu gods in the practice of *puja* (worship).

For Muslims, gardens had symbolic significance because they were seen as a miniature map of paradise. Muslim rulers divided gardens into four parts called *charbhags*, separated by water channels that represented the rivers of paradise. Gardens were so important that they inspired the designs on carpets that were made during Mughal times.

PREFERRED PLANTS
Ponds filled with aquatic plants, such as waterlilies, were much loved in both Hindu and Muslim gardens. Courtly poetry describes many varieties of lotus and waterlily. Some varieties were grown to bloom at night, by moonlight.

MOUNTAIN GARDEN
A garden, at the mountain fortress of Sigiriya in Sri Lanka, dates from around AD400. It contains the remains of enclosures and pavilions. It once had water works, including fountains, an artificial stream and a large central tank. Sigiriya is surrounded by a moat. It is said that the moat once had crocodiles in it to deter intruders.

WATERING THE PLANTS
A group of *malis* (gardeners) use an elaborate system of water courses intersecting at right angles to irrigate plants, in this Mughal period painting.

PARADISE GARDEN

A Persian-influenced carpet is woven with a design inspired by a garden. In Islam, paradise is imagined as a garden that contains the finest objects in the world. Persian carpets were usually woven into designs based on gardens.

TENDING THE GARDEN

Gardens were popular in the houses of rich and powerful people. If a household had no gardener, the women of the house were responsible for tending the garden. Usually, a garden had a mixture of flowers and useful plants, such as fruits and herbs, growing in it.

DANGEROUS PLACE

An intruder pretending to be a gardener is being threatened by the garden's owner, a noble. The painting is from the Mughal period and dates from the 1600s. In those days, the garden was a place not only of romantic but also of political intrigue. A powerful person's life could be at risk away from the house.

Weapons and Warfare

FROM ARYAN TIMES, when tribes fought among each other and stole each others' cattle, warfare was a fact of life in India. As larger empires came into being, warfare became more elaborate. By the time of the emperor Ashoka in 250BC, armies were divided into four parts – infantry (footsoldiers), cavalry (horses), chariots and elephants. The infantry was the core of all Indian armies, but was often made up of poorly trained peasants. Elephants, on the other hand, were a symbol of royalty and majesty, and gave an army great prestige.

In the 1000s, when Turks invaded, chariots became less important. This was because the Turks had excellent horses and could use bows on horseback. Soon, all Indian armies copied them and began to use high-class cavalry. The first recorded use of gunpowder was in the Deccan plateau, in central India, in the 1400s. Later, the Mughals combined field artillery (guns) with cavalry and elephants.

UNEQUAL CONTEST
A mounted warrior and a footsoldier attack each other. From the 1200s, nobles preferred to fight on horseback. Footsoldiers faced a great disadvantage in fighting men on horseback, who not only used swords, but bows as well.

SUPERIOR WARRIOR
A Mongol warrior draws his bow and aims behind him as he rides. The Mongols were great fighters, especially on horseback. In 1398, they devastated Delhi and took many of its citizens as slaves.

MUGHAL HELMET
You will need: strips of newspaper, flour and water or wallpaper paste, bowl, inflated balloon, scissors, fine sandpaper, thin card, adhesive tape or white glue, gold and black paint, paintbrushes, 20 x 10cm/8 x 4in piece of black card, ruler.

1 Soak the newspaper in the paste or flour and water. Cover half the balloon with three layers of newspaper. Leave to dry between layers.

2 When dry, burst the balloon and remove it. Smooth edges of helmet with sandpaper. Wrap a strip of card around the base. Fix with tape or glue.

3 Place a longer piece of card inside the helmet. It should be long enough to cover your ears and neck. Glue or tape it into position and trim to fit.

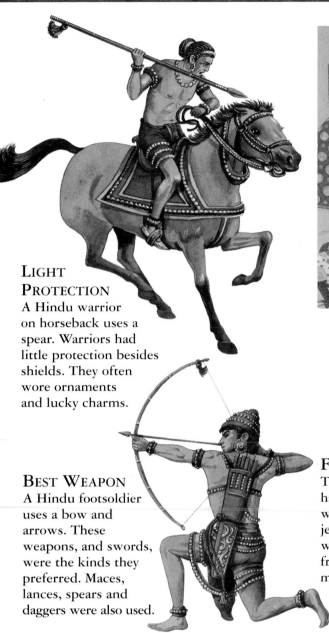

LIGHT PROTECTION
A Hindu warrior on horseback uses a spear. Warriors had little protection besides shields. They often wore ornaments and lucky charms.

BEST WEAPON
A Hindu footsoldier uses a bow and arrows. These weapons, and swords, were the kinds they preferred. Maces, lances, spears and daggers were also used.

FORTIFIED CHAIR
A king at war travels in a fortified *howdah* (chair) on an elephant's back. The combination of *howdah* and elephant was like the tank of modern warfare. The best army elephants were captured mainly in eastern and southern India, and in Sri Lanka.

FINE WEAPONRY
This Mughal dagger handle is inlaid with gold and jewels. Weapons were often crafted from the finest materials.

A Mughal warrior wore a plumed helmet to protect his head in battle.

4 Paint the entire helmet with two coats of gold paint, using a medium paintbrush. Allow the paint to dry completely between coats.

5 Add detail with black paint and a fine paintbrush. You could use a Mughal pattern like the one shown here, or design your own.

6 Cut narrow slits 5mm/¼in apart in the black card. Leave 5cm/2in uncut at the bottom of the card. Cover this patch with glue and roll the card up tightly.

7 When the glue is dry, fix the plume to the top of your helmet with glue, or you can cut a small hole in the helmet and push the plume through.

Transport and Travel

USING THE RIVERS
Boats like this one were used to travel along rivers in the north of India, such as the Ganges. The boats were steered by a large oar, instead of a rudder. Boats were particularly important for people who were traders. Ocean sailing was not a skill that was heavily developed in India.

TRAVEL BY BULLOCK CART
Carts drawn by bullocks or cows were the most common way of transporting humans and heavy loads over long distances, particularly in the countryside. Wheeled carts have been used for nearly 5,000 years, since the time of the Indus Valley civilization.

TRAVEL IN INDIA hardly changed from the beginning of the country's history until the middle of the 1800s, and journeys were a great deal longer and harder than they are today. Despite the difficulties, people had many reasons to travel and did so quite a lot. They moved from place to place to trade, to go on pilgrimages, or in times of trouble, such as during wars or famines.

Most people journeyed on foot, and used elephants, pack-oxen, horses and camels to carry their goods. Wealthier people had servants to carry loads, too. By the time of King Ashoka, around 250BC, there was a system of paths crossing plains, mountains, rivers and other geographical features. These paths had to weave around difficult or inaccessible terrain. During the monsoon, they became very muddy and sometimes were even washed away.

To overcome some of these transport problems, people used the rivers instead. This happened mainly in northern India, as the rivers in southern India were too rocky. Other people voyaged up and down the coasts. For well over 2,000 years, Indians have been very inventive and made many kinds of rafts, floats and sailing vessels.

BALANCING A LOAD

A pair of women from Rajasthan, in northern India, carry brass pots stacked one on top of the other. They are carrying water from a village well. The pots sit on cloth rings that protect the crest of the head and provide a neat cavity to secure the bottom of the pot. Bearing loads in India long ago, as today, was typically done by balancing heavy objects on the shoulders or head. This made it much easier to carry the weights because the load was spread evenly on top of the body.

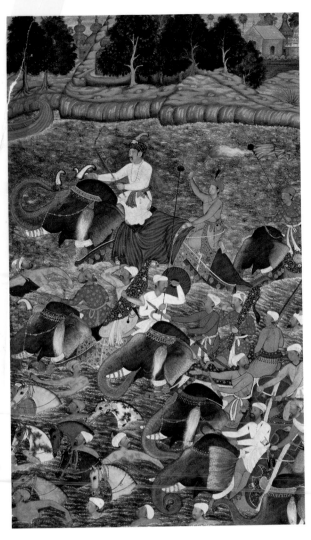

MONSOON RIVER FLOOD

Mughal forces struggle to ford a stream that has become swollen by the heavy monsoon (wet season) rains. The monsoon season in India made travel difficult. Because of this, Buddhist monks would wander in the hot dry season and settle in monasteries during the rainy season.

JOURNEYING BY CHAIR

Trumpeters announce the arrival of a Mughal prince and his wife. The royal couple are being carried in an elaborate chair known as a palanquin. Important people often journeyed in these chairs, which were carried on the shoulders of slaves or servants.

THE ADAPTABLE CAMEL

Camels were used for transport in hot, dry regions, especially in the deserts of Rajasthan and the hills of north-western India. Camels are very well adapted to extremely hot and dry conditions and are able to travel for long periods without water.

Food and Drink

EOPLE'S STAPLE (BASIC) FOOD depended on what they could grow. In the wetter areas of eastern, western, southern and central India, rice was the staple diet. In the drier areas of the north and north-west, people grew wheat and made it into different kinds of breads.

Apart from these staple foods, people's diets depended on their religion. Buddhists thought that killing animals was wrong, so they were vegetarians. Most Hindus, particularly the upper castes, became vegetarian too. Because they believed the cow was holy, eating beef became taboo (forbidden). When Islam arrived, it brought with it a new set of rules. Muslims are forbidden to eat pork, although they do eat other meat.

The Indians used a lot of spices in cooking, in order to add taste and to disguise rotten meat. Ginger, garlic, turmeric, cinnamon and cumin were used from early times. Chillis were only introduced from the Americas after the 1500s.

CELESTIAL FRUITS
A heavenly damsel offers fruits in this stucco painting from Sri Lanka. From earliest times, Indians ate with their hands rather than with implements. Even so, there were rules to be followed. Generally, they could only eat with the right hand, taking care just to use their fingers.

EVENING DELIGHTS
A princess enjoys a party in the garden. She listens to music by candlelight, and is served drinks, sweetmeats and other foods.

MAKE A CHICKPEA CURRY

You will need: knife, small onion, 30ml/2 tbsp vegetable oil, wok or frying pan, wooden spoon, 4cm/1½in piece root ginger root, 2 cloves garlic, 1.25ml/¼ tsp turmeric, 450g/ 1lb tomatoes, 225g/½lb/1½ cups cooked chickpeas, salt and pepper, 30ml/2 tbsp chopped coriander (cilantro), plus extra to garnish, 10ml/2 tsp garam masala, a lime.

1 Chop the onion finely. Heat the vegetable oil in a wok. Fry the onion in the oil for 2–3 minutes, until it is soft. Ask an adult to help you.

2 Chop the ginger finely and add to the pan. Chop the garlic cloves and add them, along with the turmeric. Cook gently for another 30 seconds.

A RICH BANQUET

Babur, the founder of the Mughal Empire in India, enjoys a banquet of exotic fruits. Under the Mughals, a cuisine known as Mughlai developed. It became famous for its rich and sophisticated tastes and aromas.

turmeric

black mustard seeds   cardamon

THREE ESSENTIAL SPICES

Turmeric is ground from a root to give food an earthy taste and yellow hue. Black mustard seed has a smoky, bitter taste. Cardamon – much loved in northern India – gives a musky, sugary taste that is suitable for all types of dishes.

LEAF PLATE

In south India, banana leaves were (and are still) used as plates for serving and eating food. South Indian food uses more coconut than the north, and rice-flour is used in several dishes.

DAILY BREAD

Indians eat a variety of baked, griddled or fried breads, such as these parathas. In much of northern and western India, the staple food is wheat, served in the form of unleavened (flat) breads.

Chickpeas are a popular ingredient in Indian cooking. They have been grown in India for thousands of years.

3 Peel the tomatoes, cut them in half and remove the seeds. Then chop them roughly and add them to the onion, garlic and spice mixture.

4 Add the chickpeas. Bring the mixture to the boil, then simmer gently for 10–15 minutes, until the tomatoes have reduced to a thick paste.

5 Taste the curry and then add salt and pepper as seasoning, if it is needed. The curry should taste spicy, but not so hot that it burns your mouth.

6 Add the chopped fresh coriander to the curry, along with the garam masala. Garnish with fresh coriander leaves and serve with slices of lime.

Festivals and Ceremonies

HANDY HENNA
Using henna to mark the hands and feet was a common custom in India, and is still part of marriage ceremonies. Henna is a plant extract that is mixed into a paste with water and used to make patterns on the skin. The paste dyes the skin red.

RITUAL CEREMONIES in India go back to Aryan times, when there were fire sacrifices throughout the year. After the growth of Buddhism, the Vedic priests developed a set of rites for important events such as marriages, caste initiations and funerals, which Hindus then used for centuries. Many temple festivals developed too. Some, such as Navaratri and Dasara, revered fierce goddesses. Diwali was a festival of lights to pay homage to the goddess Lakshmi. In spring, people played games at the fertility festival of Holi.

Generally, Muslims had fewer and less elaborate rituals. Islamic festivals included Eid al-Fitr after Ramadan, the month of fasting, and Eid al-Adha to commemorate the sacrifice of Abraham. Muslims also adopted some of the customs and customs of the Hindus.

A FESTIVAL OF FUN
The Vasantotsava (or modern Holi) was a festival of play and courtship that took place in the spring. Men and women threw bright powders and squirted dyed waters over one another with syringes as they ran about the streets and gardens of the city.

TABLA DRUM

You will need: A2 sheet of cardboard, measuring tape, scissors, pair of compasses, pencil, adhesive tape, strips of newspaper, flour and water or wallpaper paste, bowl, fine sandpaper, calico fabric, bradawl, red-brown and blue paint, paintbrushes, darning needle, twine, white glue.

1 Cut out a card rectangle 55 x 21cm/22 x 8 ½in. Cut slits along the long edges. Use the compasses to draw a card circle with a diameter of 16cm/6½in. Cut it out.

2 Roll the rectangle to form a cylinder with a diameter of 16cm/6½in and tape. Tape the slits so that the drum tapers at each end. Tape the circle to one end.

3 Cover with three layers of newspaper strips soaked in paste or flour and water. Leave it to dry between layers. Smooth the edges with sandpaper.

58

CEREMONY AROUND THE FIRE

A bride, with her face covered, is led into the marriage *pandal* (ceremonial awning), which is covered with mango and lime leaves to bring good luck. The bride will follow her husband around the fire. Hindu marriages still take place in the home around a sacrificial fire, and are administered by a Brahmin priest.

END OF FASTING

Muslim men take part in Eid festivities, in Bombay. Muslim men pray in public congregations at a mosque and give *zakat* (gifts) to the poor. Then they celebrate with friends and families.

PILGRIMAGE TO MECCA

Muslim pilgrims travel by camel to the city of Mecca, in Arabia (modern Saudi Arabia). Muslims must travel to Mecca once in their lifetime, if possible. The journey is called the haj.

DEATH OF AN IMAM

A passion play with music and drumming is enacted in the streets to celebrate Muharram, the first month of the Muslim calender. For Shia Muslims, the tenth day of Muharram is one of dramatic public mourning to commemorate the death of an imam (spiritual leader) named Husain.

The tabla *drum was played at ceremonies and festivals.*

4 Cut a circle of calico with a diameter of 25cm/10in. Prick holes around the edge with a bradawl. Paint with two coats of red-brown paint.

5 Thread the needle with a long piece of twine and knot. Place the calico over the *tabla*'s open end. Push the needle and thread through a hole in the calico.

6 Pass the twine across the base and through a hole on the other side of the fabric. Pull the twine tight, to stretch the fabric. Repeat all the way around the *tabla*.

7 Paint a pattern on to the calico. Then apply a coat of watered down white glue. This will help to shrink the calico and pull it tight over the *tabla*.

Clay and Terracotta Crafts

CLAY AND TERRACOTTA OBJECTS (known as ceramics) have played an important part in the study of Indian history, for two reasons. Making ceramics was one of India's earliest crafts. Many objects have been found at archaeological sites, dating as far back as 5000BC and the Indus Valley civilization. Also, because the objects were fired (baked), they have traces of carbon left on them, which has allowed archaeologists to date them quite accurately using a process called carbon dating.

In the Indus Valley, people made clay storage jars, terracotta seals and terracotta figurines of domestic animals. These clay animals may have been children's toys. People carried on using clay containers throughout India's history. Clay was particularly useful as it kept things cool in the hot climate. Artists also made terracotta figurines of gods and goddesses, though they gradually began to make stone and metal images as well.

RECORD IN CLAY
This terracotta cart found at Mohenjo-Daro is about 4,000 years old. Figurines like this have been found throughout the Indus valley. Although they were probably only toys, they give us information about the way people lived. For example, we can see that they were already using wheeled carts.

PAINTED POTTERY
A painted grey dish made on the Gangetic plains between 1000 and 500BC. Similar pottery was made across the region, which shows that people had contact with each other and shared the same technology.

SIMILAR STYLES
Black and red painted pottery has been found at sites dating from the Indus Valley civilization, and at later sites dating from around 500BC. It is found right across the Indian subcontinent.

MAKE A WATER POT
You will need: inflated balloon, large bowl, strips of newspaper, flour and water or wallpaper paste, scissors, fine sandpaper, strip of corrugated cardboard, adhesive tape, terracotta and black paint, paintbrushes, pencil, white glue.

1 Cover the balloon with four layers of newspaper soaked in paste. When dry, cut a slit in the papier mâché. Remove the balloon. Add more layers to give the pot a tapered top.

2 Roll the corrugated cardboard into a circle shape to fit on to the narrow end of the pot to form a base. Fix the base in place with adhesive tape.

3 Cover the corrugated cardboard base with four layers of soaked newspaper. Leave to dry beween each layer. Smooth the edges with sandpaper.

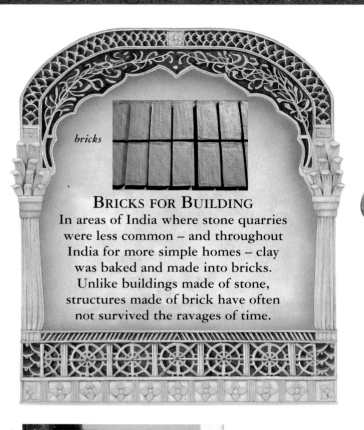

BRICKS FOR BUILDING

bricks

In areas of India where stone quarries were less common – and throughout India for more simple homes – clay was baked and made into bricks. Unlike buildings made of stone, structures made of brick have often not survived the ravages of time.

TERRACOTTA GODDESS

A female terracotta figure found in Mathura, Uttar Pradesh. It may be an image of a mother goddess. Many terracotta images were made during the Mauryan period (400–200BC) and immediately afterwards. They were cheaper versions of the stone sculptures that were built at the imperial court.

THROWING A POT

A village potter shapes a clay vessel as it spins on his potter's wheel. Pottery was an important part of the ancient urban and village economies and is still practised in India today. Clay used for making pottery is available in most parts of the land.

Clay water pots that are 4,000 years old have been found in the Indus Valley. People carried the pots on their heads.

4 When it is dry, paint the water pot with two coats of terracotta paint, to make it look as though it is made of terracotta. Leave to dry between coats.

5 Draw some patterns on the water pot with a pencil. Copy the ancient Indian pattern shown here, or create your own individual design.

6 Carefully paint your designs using black paint and a fine paintbrush. Keep the edges of your lines neat and clean. Leave to dry.

7 Add final details, again using a fine paintbrush. When the paint is dry, seal the surface of the water pot with a coat of watered down white glue.

Glossary

A

archaeology The study of ancient remains and ruins.

Aryans A group of people who migrated into India around 1500BC.

ascetics Monks or religious wanderers who rejected home life to pursue enlightenment.

B

barter To exchange one item for another, without money.

bodhi tree Symbol of the Buddha. The tree he sat under when he achieved enlightenment.

Brahmi An ancient Indian script.

Brahmins The priests, members of the first caste.

Buddha A prince who abandoned his family to seek enlightenment. Founder of the Buddhist way of life.

C

caste One of four social classes into which Hindus were divided.

chauri A whisk, usually made of yak tail, for fanning away flies.

citadel Fortress near to or inside a city.

civilization A society that has made advances in arts, science and technology, law or government.

collyrium A black paste used as eyeliner.

conch A type of large, vibrant sea shell.

courtier Person attending at royal court.

cowrie A seashell used as the lowest form of currency near the coastal regions of Ancient India.

D

dargah Shrine to a sufi saint.

deity A god or goddess.

dhoti Traditional Indian dress worn by Hindu men.

discus A heavy disc, symbol of the god Vishnu.

E

edict Order issued by a king.

Eid al-Fitr Celebration at the end of the month of fasting in Islam.

empire A large number of different lands ruled over by a single person or government.

enlightenment Freedom from ignorance through meditation. Buddhist monks try to achieve enlightenment.

epic Long poem telling a story.

F

frieze Decorated strip along a wall or ceiling.

G

Ganesha Elephant-headed Hindu god. He is lord of Shiva's armies.

gopuram Gate tower of a south Indian temple.

gurdwara Sikh place of worship.

H

haj Pilgrimage to Mecca that a Muslim should make at least once.

Hanuman Leader of the monkey army that helps Rama rescue Sita in the *Ramayana*.

Hinduism Religion that includes worship of several gods and belief in reincarnation.

Holi A festival celebrating the onset of spring in Ancient India.

hookah Water pipe used to smoke tobacco.

I

incarnation Human form of god.

irrigation Bringing water to dry lands so that crops can be grown.

Islam Religion of Muslim people.

J

jama Side-fastening coat worn with trousers in Mughal times.

jataka A story telling of a previous birth of the Buddha.

K

Kali A fierce form of Shiva's wife.

kangha A comb, one of the five objects carried by Sikh brotherhoods.

Kaurava One of the two feuding families of the *Mahabharata*.

Krishna Vaishnava god who forms the main character in the *Mahabharata*.

Kshatriya A warrior, a member of the second caste.

M

mace Spiked club used by Hindu warriors.

Mahabharata A story of the contest for succession between the families of the Kauravas and Pandavas.

makara A mythical crocodile-like animal.

mausoleum A very grand tomb.

medieval Relating to the period from about AD500–1500.

minar A tower next to a mosque.

mortar Mixture used to stick bricks or stones together.

mosque A Muslim place of worship.

Muharram First month of the Muslim calender.

Muslim A follower of the prophet Mohammed.

myth An ancient story of gods and heroes.

N

Nagari The modern alphabet of north Indian languages.

nirvana Freedom from suffering.

O

omen A sign of good or bad fortune in the future.

P

paijama Tight-fitting trousers worn during Mughal times.

palanquin A seat or carriage carried on the shoulders of men.

Pandava One of the two feuding families of the *Mahabharata*.

paratha A fried wheat bread eaten in northern India.

patron Person who gives money and encouragement to the arts.

Persian Language spoken in Persia. It came to be used by the Muslim nobility who ruled India.

pilgrim Person who makes a journey to a holy place.

polo A game, similar to hockey, played on horseback.

puja Revering an icon of a god.

R

Radha The best-loved of lord Krishna as a youth.

raja Indian king or prince.

Rama The hero-king of the *Ramayana*.

Ramayana The story of Rama's rescue of his wife Sita from the demon Ravana.

Ravana Demon who is the villain of the *Ramayana*.

S

Sanskrit Language of the Aryans. The language of the ruling classes in Ancient India.

sari Traditional female Indian dress.

sceptre Ceremonial staff carried by a king.

Shaivism Belief in Shiva as the lord of the Universe.

shalwar kamiz Long tunic and trousers worn in nothern India.

Shia A branch of Islam.

shikar A hunting expedition.

Shiva A chief Hindu god.

shrine Sacred place of worship.

Shudra Servant or peasant, member of the lowest caste.

sitar Guitar-like instrument.

soapstone A soft mineral.

stupa Buddhist place of worship containing a relic of the Buddha.

Sufism Mystical form of Islam.

sultan A Muslim ruler.

T

tabla Drum played in north Indian classical music.

terracotta Reddish-brown unglazed earthenware.

textile Cloth produced by weaving threads together.

turban Headdress worn by Muslim, Sikh and some Hindu men.

V

Vaishnavism Belief in Vishnu as the lord of the Universe.

Vishnu A chief Hindu god.

Veda Ancient Aryan texts relating to religion.

Vaishya Merchant or farmer, a member of the third caste.

Y

Yaksi A female tree spirit.

Z

zakat Alms that must be given to the poor in Islam.

Index

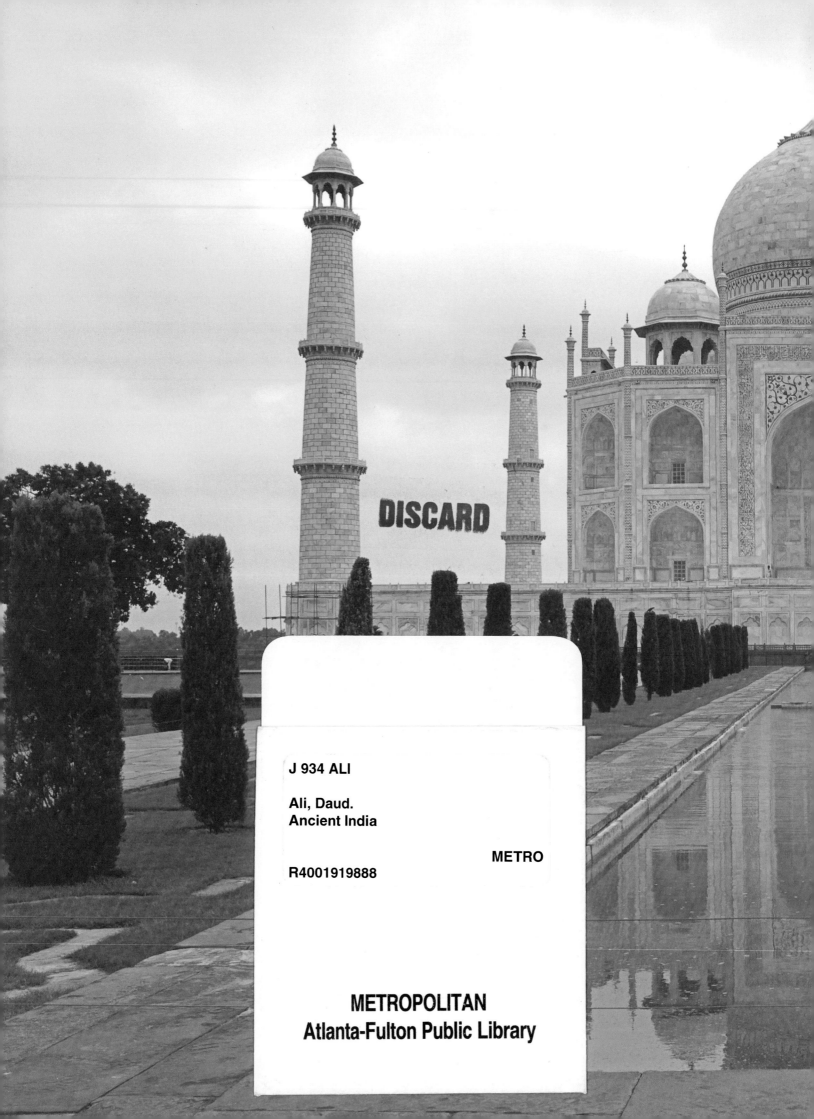